Other Books by T. R. Fehrenbach

The Battle of Anzio
United States Marines in Action
Crisis in Cuba
This Kind of War
This Kind of Peace
The Swiss Banks
Crossroads in Korea
F.D.R.'s Undeclared War: 1939–1941
The United Nations in War and Peace
Lone Star

The second day of July, 1776, will be the most memorable epoch in the history of America. I am apt to believe that it will be celebrated by succeding generations as the great anniversary festival. It ought to be commemorated as the day of deliverance, by solemn acts of devotion to God Almighty. It ought to be solemnized with pomp and parade, with shows, games, sports, guns, bells, bonfires and illuminations, from one end of this continent to the other, from this time forward, forevermore.

You will think me transported with enthusiasm, but I am not. I am well aware of the toil, and blood, and treasure, that it will cost us to maintain this declaration, and support and defend these States. Yet, through all the gloom, I can see rays of ravishing light and glory. I can see that the end is more than worth all the means, and that posterity will triumph in that day's transaction, even although we should rue it, which I trust in God we shall not.

John Adams to Abigail Adams, July 3, 1776

T. R. FEHRENBACH

Greatness To Spare

The heroic sacrifices
of the men who signed
the Declaration of Independence

D. VAN NOSTRAND COMPANY, INC.
Princeton, New Jersey Toronto London Melbourne

Foreword

Most Americans and many citizens of the world consider the American Declaration of Independence the foremost statement of human rights and democratic principles of government ever written. It is well known that John Adams of Massachusetts assigned Thomas Jefferson of Virginia the task of writing this monumental document, and in it Jefferson not only projected his own genius but summed up the highest American aspirations of the day.

But nobody really knows the other men who sat with Thomas Jefferson in Philadelphia in 1776; who debated, voted for, and finally signed the Declaration. Who were they? What motivated them to declare Independence, and what did they hope to gain? Above all, what did they risk? And finally, what happened to these men? What did they get out of it? That is what this book is all about.

Each generation rewrites history to suit its current beliefs and biases. Eighteenth- and nineteenth-century American historians generally held different viewpoints and certainly different social biases from the majority of researchers writing now. Today the viewpoint is increasingly that of the specialist, yet it is difficult to find five specialists who agree on every point. I have deliberately relied as much on older accounts as on the new.

I also have my own viewpoints and biases. I admire Richard Henry Lee with unabashed emotion and believe in what he stood for, and I love the kind of man typified by Thomas Nelson, Jr. Also, I take deep pride in the fact that the sensible American leadership never allowed the Revolutionary War against Great Britain to sink into a socially disastrous American Revolution. In such a case, liberties could hardly have been preserved, and I believe that these men intended to preserve liberty *and* property, finding nothing antithetical between the two. I believe the American Revolution was not so much a great popular uprising as a controlled experiment in freedom conducted by men whose motives were primarily moral and ideological and patriotic—and all the early writers believed the same.

Whenever possible, dates and other concrete data have been checked against accepted authorities. Several incidents about the Signers are unprovable, or doubtful. For example, Elbridge Gerry could not have talked about "dancing on air" with Benjamin Harrison at the Signing; they were not both in Philadelphia on August 2, 1776. But the remark was probably made at some other time. The Congress deliberately veiled some of its doings in secrecy, and older chroniclers ignore chronology.

This emphasis is also my own. A multi-biography presents problems enough without trying to cover all fifty-six men. I have concentrated on what happened to the Congress after signing, and I have narrowed the field in other respects also. The careers of Thomas Jefferson, Benjamin Franklin, and John Adams are too well known to need elaboration. An accident of history confined the major British operations to the Middle Atlantic and Southern states after 1776. Therefore, I have largely left out the New Englanders.

This omission is not an attempt to scant or denigrate the men of New England. They were exactly the same kind of men at heart and took exactly the same risks as the others. Many of them took risks earlier; Massachusetts was first in rebellion. John Hancock lost approximately $100,000, then a great fortune, through investing his assets in Continental money; another New England Signer was wounded in battle. But the majority were not required to redeem in burnt houses and blood their pledges made at Philadelphia.

Nor is this book intended to be a detailed history of the Revolutionary War itself. I have not quoted extensively from any scholar or from anyone except the men of the times themselves.

My only purpose has been to show what the Signers did, what they risked, and what the signing cost them. If their ordeals were relevant then they are surely relevant now, and they have certainly been too long ignored.

July, 1968

T.R.F.

Contents

THE CONGRESS

Bid Defiance

On the seventh of June, 1776, a slender, keen-eyed Virginian named Richard Henry Lee rose in the State House, off Chestnut Street in Philadelphia, where the Second Continental Congress of the thirteen colonies of British America sat. Lee put a brief proposition before the house:

RESOLVED, *That these United Colonies are, and of right ought to be, free and independent States, that they are absolved from all allegiance to the British Crown, and that all political connection between them and the State of Great Britain is, and ought to be, totally dissolved.*

That it is expedient forthwith to take the most effectual measures for forming foreign alliances.

That a plan of confederation be prepared and transmitted to the respective Colonies for their consideration and approbation.

The reluctance of the Congress to adopt the motion is well known. Until this time, the dominant view of the resistance leaders in America was that they were British subjects fighting an oppressive Parliament for their inherent rights as Englishmen, a view almost all British historians

to the World

have supported. A declaration of independence was then an overt recognition of something few men completely understood: that over the course of one hundred and fifty years, Great Britain and British America had actually become separate, and different, countries; Americans were not simply Englishmen born abroad; and that the British government was not now, nor ever, prepared to make a decent compromise on American grievances. Up till now, although blood had wetted Breed's Hill, the Colonies had raised an army and appointed a commander-in-chief, had driven the royal governors to British warships off the coast, and had authorized attacks on the high seas of British sail, Americans could still claim to be His Majesty's "loyal opposition"; every petition and document sent to the government of Great Britain professed American loyalty to the King. The Crown was, and always had been, the symbol of sovereignty, legitimacy, law, and social order in America. It—and the British connection—was not taken lightly by thinking men, and the idea that both should be cast off was strongly resisted, even after the British and Americans had

3

gone to war. Between 1773 and 1775, the vast majority of Americans had never planned to make a genuine revolution; they had hoped only to secure a return to the *status quo ante* of 1763, before Crown officers began to regulate commerce efficiently, Whitehall tried to control the western lands, and Parliament insisted upon taxing Americans without representation. The intransigence of the British Ministry on all questions, and the policy of overawing disobedience by troops and force, had precipitated civil war. The realization that the American Revolution was also a genuine national war was slow in coming, because of history, sentiment, legalisms, prudence, and plain wishful thinking.

The ringing debate and tumultuous parliamentary maneuvers of the next few days and weeks, when, as elegant young Edward Rutledge of South Carolina wrote fellow moderate, John Jay of New York, *The sensible part of the house opposed the motion,* and Lee, the Adamses and John Hancock of Massachusetts, and Virginians and Georgians worked on the floor and behind the scenes to pass it, are not part of this story. After four days of debate, the motion carried, by one vote. Then, on a motion by Edward Rutledge, the whole question was deferred until July 1, and many delegates hoped it had been put off forever.

But, as the evidence shows, the countryside was clearly ahead of the Congress. Independence, as John Adams wrote, was rolling like a torrent over the land. British policy inflamed the people. The Royal Navy, for no good reason, disembarked troops at Falmouth (in what is now Maine) and burned the town. The deposed Royal Governor of Virginia, John Murray, Earl of Dunmore, ordered Norfolk bombarded, and tried to cause an insurrection among the Negro slaves. King's officers stirred up Indian troubles in the West, causing massacres of colonists. It became known that the British Ministry had hired Hessian mercenaries for American service. All of these measures indicated a monarch more concerned with cowing his American subjects than compromising their grievances, and collectively they were fatal to the moderate cause.

Between June 7 and July 1, the assembly of colony after colony instructed its representatives at Philadelphia to support a declaration of independence. Events crowded the Congress. Still, when the crucial vote was taken on July 2, and it was obvious that it would carry, only a significant feeling for American solidarity allowed the balloting to be unanimous. Four delegates, unable to vote against their conscience, resigned. Two, John Dickinson and Robert Morris of Pennsylvania, deliberately stayed away so that their colonial delegation could show a majority for independence. The New York delegation, lukewarm at best for breaking the ties, had received no instruction from home. It did not vote for independence, but chose not to obstruct and vote against it.

After four hot, sweaty, tumultuous days in July, the presiding officer of Congress, John Hancock, signed Thomas Jefferson's great manifesto on the evening of the fourth. Charles Thomson, Secretary, attested. On this date no one else signed.

Four days afterward, on July 8, *freedom was proclaimed throughout the land.* This was no longer opposition to Parliament; it was revolution against the British Crown and Empire. It was also treason under every law and concept of the time, and every delegate who voted for it knew it.

The Declaration was a great statement of American principle, and as such it was welcomed from colony to colony. It was read to cheering crowds in Philadelphia, summoned by the Liberty Bell. General George Washington, at New York, ordered it read to the brigades of the Continental Army drawn up in hollow squares at evening. While the General sat impassively on his grey horse, the Army cheered.

In all the towns from North to South there was tumult and excitement as the proclamation was received and understood. Newport, Williamsburg, and Charleston held mass meetings, conducted public prayers, and celebrated with gala balls. Everywhere the symbols of British sovereignty—the Union Jack over the assembly houses, the King's arms, and the King's effigy—were torn or trampled down. In some places there were riotous scenes, and statues of George III were toppled and melted for bullets; in others, British symbols were removed in impressive ceremonies with fife and drum.

Avowed Loyalists or Tories stayed in their homes. The eager, widespread acceptance of the Declaration of Independence shows that the American feeling of territoriality was very strong, and this sentiment far outran the cautious conservatism of the delegates sent to Congress. But as Adams wrote, and the Congress collectively knew, a mere declaration of independence did not make the colonies free. George III, in a letter to Lord North, the Prime Minister, had summed it up succinctly in 1774: *Blows must decide whether they are to be subject to this country or independent.*

Many members of Congress, understanding the dangers of all-out war with the power of Great Britain, to the last had hoped to achieve a livable compromise and avoid **the**

6

coming blows. The patriotism of none of these men has been questioned. Rutledge, John Jay of New York, John Dickinson, Robert Morris, and James Wilson of Pennsylvania, Carter Braxton of Virginia, and George Read of Delaware, among many others, stood foursquare with the American cause; most of them had been among the early leaders in the opposition to British acts and encroachments. Some of them held out only because of timing—believing that independence should be held back to use as a bargaining point later on. Others sincerely believed that, although Americans must fight to the knife for their inherent rights against Great Britain, they should try to stay within the empire. There was inherent peril in any revolution, any breakage of the laws. As Gouverneur Morris wrote, *I see, and I see with fear and trembling that if the disputes with Great Britain continue, we shall be under the domination of a riotous mob. . . .* It was never far from the Congress' mind that the same people joyously tearing down the symbols of British law and order today could easily turn to closer symbols and leaders as well.

The secret journals of the Congress reveal that the Declaration of Independence was ordered to be engrossed on parchment on July 19, 1776, so that there could be a symbolic signing by the delegates. The day set for the signing was August 2.

Not all the men who voted for independence in July could be present for the ceremony. Some, including Oliver Wolcott of Connecticut and Thomas McKean of Delaware, were away with the army; they signed later. Others had left the Congress entirely, and were not authorized to sign. There were also a number of newly-arrived delegates, who had not been present on July 2 and 4, who now signed their names to the document. At least one man who had voted against it (the unanimous vote was by state delegations, not within those delegations) now signed; this was George Read of Delaware. And Robert Morris, the merchant prince of Philadelphia, who had stayed away from the sessions in order to avoid voting no, now signed also.

If the vote taken on July 2 could be construed by posterity as a momentous act of patriotism, the men who assembled in State House a month later were painfully aware that to put their signatures on this piece of parchment was to give permanent evidence of high treason. It was one thing to vote during a period of brilliant oratory and high drama with the winning side; it was quite another to sign a document denying the sovereign power of the British Crown, which had been the symbol of authority for these men all their lives. This was not a mere protest petition, protected by a firm concept of civil rights. It was an act of high treason, for which the universal penalty was death by hanging. For that reason, there was a grim determination to the signing ceremony and, also, more than one instance of gallows humor among the Congress that day.

This was undoubtedly the most remarkable body of revolutionaries ever to assemble anywhere. They wore silken stocks, wigs or powdered hair, silk stockings, and many were clad in velvet breeches and brilliantly colored coats. They met in the Assembly Room, on the east side of the entrance hallway. The day was very hot, and lengthy preliminaries were dispensed with. Charles Thomson, the Congress' Secretary, set up the Declaration on a table, and the fifty-some delegates present came forward by states to sign. Observers said later that they were both serious and affable.

John Hancock of Massachusetts had described this Congress in the following words: *Here are fortunes, abilities, learning, eloquence, acuteness, equal to any I ever met in my life.* Now, the men who represented all this stepped forward to lay all of it on the line—to pledge their lives, fortunes, and sacred honor with the pen, for the sake of the country they had just declared.

What kind of men were these fifty-six, who in Congress assembled represented some two and a half million American freemen? Where did they come from, and how and why did they get here at this time? In the answer to these questions lie some of the most significant keys to the American Revolution, and the foundation of the nation.

Noticeably, the Signers were young; eighteen were still in their thirties, and three were in their twenties. Benjamin Franklin, of Pennsylvania, was the only really old man present. All these men still had a lifetime to live.

Almost all this group, with the exception of Samuel Adams of Massachusetts, owned substantial property. Adams' friends had bought him a new suit and a horse and given him a little pocket money so he would be presentable in this assemblage. Eleven delegates were prosperous merchants; one owned the best-known and largest mercantile house in the colonies. Nine were large landowners, and their holdings included some of the greatest estates in America. When these men wrote the word "fortune" in their pledge, it was no idle boast.

Twenty-four representatives, including some who pursued other careers as well, were lawyers or jurists. The rest of the fifty-six other professional men, doctors of medicine, a divine, or career politicians, and merchants. All of these men knew that if Great Britain won this struggle, whether they hung or not, they would not likely practice again.

All but two had wives and children at home. A considerable number still had infant children; almost all these families were exposed to British action up and down the long coast.

All of these eighteenth-century Americans came from what would later be called the "power structure"; each was prominent or influential in some way in his own locality. Many had reputations that reached across colonial borders, or like Franklin's, to Europe. But whatever their own part in the power structure of colonial America, the delegates did not have much real power behind them. They were no longer quite the mere extra-legal assembly of individual men the First Continental Congress had been; they had been expressly sent to represent their colonial assemblies in united action, and for the most part they had been most carefully chosen. Almost every assembly or legislature had sensed crucial decisions would be made in 1775 and 1776 at Philadelphia. All had sent their most capable, patriotic, and representative men. But these delegates did not represent a truly united or powerful nation; they represented little power, and even less power to command. They were really only delegates to a confederate congress from thirteen newly-sovereign but shaky state governments; they could authorize, but not direct. They had authorized an army, and appointed General Washington to command it, but as every American knows, they did not then or later have the power to raise taxes to support it. The American cause had to rely on volunteers in the Army, and voluntary support by civilians everywhere.

On the day of signing, the Continental Army stood at about 10,000 men, under Washington at New York. Other than that, there was only the militia of the several states, brave men, but badly armed and worse trained, of doubtful quality in the face of British bayonets. The Congress had already received word from General Washington of a vast flotilla—dozens of sail, 42,000 seamen and soldiers altogether—standing off Sandy Hook. The largest body of armed men ever sent to North America was about to land to crush the Revolution. The Crown had promised amnesty to any Americans who renounced the rebel cause, and severity to those who did not. Behind that armada in the Atlantic was the world's greatest empire, a wealthy and powerful nation of nine million people who ruled the seas.

No man, however prominent at home, could sign the Declaration in perfect safety, or hope to sit out the ensuing war. There were several delegates lining up before Secretary Thomson's table who in their hearts doubted if the colonies could win. The real battle was not yet joined; the issue was much in doubt.

At this time and at this place, it was reasonably certain that every man in this hall had more to lose from this Revolution than he could possibly hope to gain—except for honor and principle. The resistance to Parliament had begun over duties, lands, and taxation—property—but it had rapidly become a stand for principle. The taxes that Parliament had imposed on America did bite some severely, expecially the Stamp Tax, but that had already been repealed. The tea tax, part of an ingenious plan to aid the East India Company consume a surplus and assert the right of Parliament to tax at the same time, actually lowered the American cost of tea. Taxes of this kind, also, could not really affect the immensely wealthy landowners who were so influential here. But they were seen as an opening wedge. They were an assertion of the potential power to destroy, and they were opposed, at the risk of life, limb, and fortune, on principle. This was an attitude and a resolve the British Ministry never quite understood. Knowledgeable men in Britain argued with exasperation that the taxes levied did not really hurt America—and thus avoided the entire point.

When the propertied delegates attached their names to the Declaration, they made all their possessions, as traitors, forfeit. If they were seeking merely to preserve their property, the better part of valor would have been to sit this riotous summer out to see who would win.

This was a peculiarly ethical gentry who represented—in fact who first declared—the United States. They were a phenomenon of their age and place. They were not representative of the entire mass of the American people; they were an admitted élite. There is tremendous evidence that while, culturally, the American seacoast lagged a hundred years behind Western Europe, the American population in the New World had become the most generally prosperous, free, and politically progressive people in the eighteenth-century world. In these things, and in the small, ethical, and inherently liberal élite the British colonies threw up, from Massachusetts to Georgia, America could be said to be far ahead of Europe and the British Isles. Although the laws, customs, and ethics of America were inherited from the British, in the open lands and almost unlimited opportunity of the Atlantic frontier something new had developed. If Americans were culturally crude in the mass, and few men were rich in European terms, still most men could read and write, and poverty—in the grinding, terrible European sense—almost did not exist. Most men owned property of some kind; real property then was within virtually the reach of all. There were no legal or social restrictions placed on anyone, with the exception of bond servants, temporarily, and the Negro slaves.

Out of this milieu came a strong push toward self-government, through local assemblies, which the Crown had often resisted, but even more often tolerated or accepted. By the middle of the eighteenth century, these colonial legislatures, which were based on British law but really constituted an American creation, ran internal affairs. The royal governors signed their acts and carried them out under the executive authority of the Crown. Sometimes the governors disallowed the acts of local legislatures; a certain amount of friction was inevitable. But only when the governors were directed to enforce unpopular acts of Parliament, against public opposition and the will of the several assemblies, did genuine crisis come about. The royal governors, more often than not, exercised the royal authority with political wisdom and tact. When the hardening attitudes in England forced them to stand adamant, to uphold British authority to rule the colonies and enforce unpopular laws, the system rapidly broke down. Americans had developed remarkably free institutions in their assemblies—and had no intention of sacrificing them.

The seats in the various colonial legislatures of the eighteenth century were normally filled by election at large, but there were certain striking differences from later times. Society everywhere in America were predominantly rural, and mercantile or agricultural. It was rather simple, with a limited number of occupations and gradations. It is not too great an oversimplification to describe it in the terms the contemporary Virginians used: gentlemen and yeoman, mechanics and slaves. Although there were variations from colony to colony, generally all freeholders, which included the vast majority of yeoman farmers, tradesmen, and "mechanics," were entitled to the franchise. There were instances where the property requirement was overlooked or not enforced as well. While the franchise laws seem restrictive, the effective electorate seems to have been as large as in later times. Roman Catholics were disenfranchised but there were fewer than 30,000 in all America. Only men of property could vote, but the ownership of small plots of ground and houses, seems to have been far more widespread then than later, after the population grew and became urbanized.

If the yeoman farmers made up the great bulk of the communities North and South, the gentry was an easily distinguishable group. It was not a class or aristocracy by law, though there were laws of entail and primogeniture in several colonies, to hold estates intact. The "gentry" was composed of men or the descendents of men who had become successful landowners, merchants, or professionals at medicine or law. There was a tendency for rich landowners to engage in trade, and for successful merchants to buy landed estates; thus the two groups overlapped far more than in later times. The gentry were distinguished by their fine homes, relative wealth, and, as much as anything else, by their way of life. It was a tradition for gentlemen to engage in public affairs, to be lavishly hospitable, and to take the lead in forming public opinion on matters of the day. This was a vastly different ethic from the one that arose to dominance in America after industrialism; the gentry of the eighteenth century were not merely "the idle rich," or men engaged to the exclusion of all else in their personal affairs.

A marked characteristic of early American society was its "deferential" quality: generally, all classes deferred to the gentry in the management of public affairs. It was virtually demanded of men of prominent families that they serve as magistrates or in local legislatures; at the same time, it was generally agreed that only this type of man should be sent to represent the communities. There was absolutely no restriction by class as to such service. But generally it was unpaid; the professional politician was largely an invention of the nineteenth century in America; and the yeomen of New England, as well as Virginia, preferred to choose their delegates or assemblymen from prominent families. Ancestry, present status, and personal accomplishment all weighed heavily. A George Washington, returned to Burgesses many times through "cheerful, rumpot elections," made up for his middle-class origins through growing wealth and prominence as Virginia's first soldier during the French and Indian War; a Patrick Henry traded on his wit and eloquence as well as standing at law; while a Carter or a Harrison usually could win election if he merely stood. This system, universal to some degree, threw a remarkable amount of talent and merit into the colonial legislatures. Since the assemblies in turn chose the Continental Congresses when the Revolution began, a very real American élite reached the top.

This élite, of which a continuing proportion was self-made, ran local affairs in the Colonies, just as some similar élite, however chosen, managed affairs in every organized society. Few of these men thought of themselves as a class, as such, though they did recognize each other as an élite. Significantly, although the social arrogance of the gentry occasionally rubbed lesser citizenry the wrong way, the gentry did not really oppress or impinge on anyone—with significant exceptions in Pennsylvania and North Carolina, where deep tensions between controlling financial interests and western backwoodsmen had arisen. The notion of aristocracy, though it frequently crops up, seems to have been essentially foreign. Although Americans, then and later, often used the term "aristocrat" loosely, there were men, such as the Lees and Harrisons, whom this term fitted. But the system as a whole was more squirearchical than aristocratic, and in fact, the majority of American gentry had a real distaste for genuine aristocracy. The reason was not hard to find. Britain, the mother country, had an aristocratic society in the main, and the fact barred most Americans from honors or high office in the Empire. Washington could not secure the King's commission as a youth, though it was his dearest wish to be a soldier of the King. Arthur Middleton and his family and others with baronial American estates, were not easily presented at court. The most honored offices in America went to members of the tiny English aristocracy far more often than to men of proven merit.

There was, among the élite, a strong oligarchical sentiment. If it was open-ended, accepting merit, the élite also strongly felt that men should prove themselves before trying to assume leadership. It was Washington's boast that he gave every man his due, but not one farthing more, and this underlying oligarchical trait was noticeable everywhere. If the American gentry was remarkably ethical on the whole, it was also pragmatic and rather short on sentiment. Jefferson was brilliant, but hardly the norm.

The men who queued up in Congress to sign the Declaration came almost entirely from this breed, North, Middle Atlantic, and South. To an amazing extent, despite many personal differences of opinion, they spoke the same language and understood the same symbology; they were products of a similar social background and process. They were instinctively non-ideological in their approach to law or life. They were all acknowledged leaders in their communities, and in most cases, had had experience at local government. They were men with a deep stake in their colonies, both of property and prestige. They were rarely impetuous or rash, though this type of gentleman did exist. They were conservative socially, while inherently liberal in their deepest concepts of society and law. In short, they were a peculiarly American, and easily recognizable American leadership.

During all the debates, the great majority felt an extreme reluctance to step off into the unknown. They had a painful fear that their own actions, in breaking the existing law, would inflame the "riotous mob"—there was a continual pull between the need to arouse the public against the British and the dread that the resistance would get out of hand. There was very little kindling, fiery momentum, or the rush to extremism found in most revolutions. There was, instead, a profound respect for the law, and a selective breaking of it only. Few rebels were ever so conservative, cautious, worldly-wise, or so afraid of their own rebellion. They were not, from the evidence, afraid for themselves.

William Ellery of Rhode Island, Harvard Class of 1747 and a Newport lawyer, wanted to see everything that happened on the signing day. He moved in close to the table and stood where he had a good view of each Signer's face. He wanted to record, for posterity, *how they all looked as they signed what might be their death warrants.* He *eyed each man closely,* and wrote simply, *Undaunted resolution was displayed in every countenance.*

The richly attired John Hancock, President of Congress,

signed his name in huge, shaded letters. Hancock had inherited a large mercantile fortune, and he had been living elegantly in England when George III ascended the throne. But he had been one of the first Massachusetts men to defy the royal governor of the colony. When the old colonial assembly had formed itself into a Provincial Congress, Hancock had been chosen to preside over it. Under his leadership, Massachusetts Bay moved steadily toward resistance, appointing a Committee of Safety and drilling 12,000 minutemen. With Samuel Adams, John Hancock was marked down as a rebel and traitor to the Crown.

The march of redcoats from Boston to Lexington on April 18 and 19, 1775, actually had a twofold purpose. One was to seize the militia's military stores; the other was to arrest Hancock and Adams. Warned by Paul Revere, the two resistance leaders had to be dissuaded from joining the minutemen on the village green; they were considered too valuable to the American cause. They had been urged to leave Lexington, and they had ridden out with the sounds of the militia's fife and drum in their ears.

After the outbreak of fighting around Boston, only these two were specifically excluded from the general amnesty offered by the British. The Crown went further; it offered a reward of £500 for the capture of either man.

After he had signed, Hancock looked at the enormous signature on the parchment and grinned: *There! His Majesty can now read my name without spectacles, and can now double his reward of five hundred pounds for my head. That is my defiance!*

Then, as he backed away from the table, Hancock said, *We must be unanimous. There must be no pulling different ways; we must all hang together.*

Old Benjamin Franklin's eyes twinkled. The man who had started out as a printer's devil and was now the most widely known man in America, said: *Yes. We must all hang together, or most assuredly we shall all hang separately.*

Benjamin Harrison of Virginia, a large, heavy, jovial man, joked with the birdlike Elbridge Gerry of Massachusetts, *With me, it will all be over in a minute. But you, you'll be dancing on air an hour after I'm gone.* Gerry's reply was not recorded.

Stephen Hopkins of Rhode Island, Ellery's colleague, took up the pen and tried to put it to the parchment. His hand shook. Handing the quill to Ellery, who was next to sign, he said angrily, *My hand trembles, but my heart does not!* Hopkins was past sixty, the second oldest signer after Franklin, and suffered from palsy.

Hancock inquired of a newly-arrived delegate from Maryland, who had not been in Congress to vote the Declaration, if he would sign. *Most willingly*, the Marylander said. He was Charles Carroll, a clear-eyed man of the world, an expert swordsman and graceful dancer. Educated in Europe, Carroll was the only millionaire and sole Roman Catholic in Congress.

He wrote "Charles Carroll of Carrollton" on the Declaration. This was the only signature that contained more than a simple name, and it was Carroll's normal way of signing, to distinguish himself from his father and relatives of the same name. Carrollton was the name of his magnificent manor in Maryland. The tale that he signed this particular way so the British would know which Carroll to hang was a fiction; he had used the style for some years. He was considered the richest man in all America. When he put down the pen, some unknown member of the Congress was heard to whistle softly: *There go a few millions!*

Carroll had much, in terms of money, to lose. When he signed, Carroll, along with the other Marylanders, felt particularly vulnerable to British retaliation. The families and estates of Charles Carroll, William Paca, Samuel Chase, and Thomas Stone were all situated on Chesapeake Bay, patrolled and controlled by the Royal Navy. Each of these men, however, had been instrumental in persuading the Maryland assembly to opt for independence, and the first three willingly signed the Declaration now.

Carter Braxton of Virginia, who had opposed the Declaration as premature, and who had been added to the "radical" Virginia delegation to express this sentiment in Congress by the element who thought the same at home, also signed without protest. Braxton believed he must stand with the other Americans, as a gesture of solidarity. Braxton, a wealthy planter, had just invested heavily in a merchant fleet sailing under the British flag. He knew what his signature might cost him.

The four South Carolinians were all youthful planters and lawyers. They had put up a considerable battle against the Declaration despite the fact that the new South Carolina Assembly had come out for it; then as now, it was not uncommon for American elected representatives to follow their own consciences rather than home sentiment. They had, for better or worse, been instrumental in excising Thomas Jefferson's original censures on Negro slavery from the document. Now, they signed with grace and humor. All four had been educated in England. Rich and elegant, they tended to be distrustful of what they considered the New Englanders' "leveling spirit," because each of them represented a baronial way of plantation life. Like the New York delegation, the South Carolinians were dubious of casting aside the hierarchical symbol of the Crown; they wanted some anchor, some social rock of tradition; they were not quite sure where the revolutionary spirit would lead. Still, they signed; they were Americans, caught up in a common purpose from Charleston to Massachusetts Bay. The New Englanders, enthusiastic to break off from Great Britain, felt, in return that the Carolinians, like the Marylanders, were too much given to the pleasures and practicalities of the world, but these personal prejudices on each side were subdued in the deliberate search for solidarity.

The delegates from New York, who had abstained from voting for the Declaration because their new government at home had not ratified independence until after Congress publicly proclaimed it, were the men most deeply aware of imminent retribution on this second of August. Washington's expresses on the arrival of the British fleet had alarmed them for their families' safety. All had homes and other property exposed to British invasion, or Tory retaliation—and the Tory party was strong in New York. All these men signed without comment, but also without hesitation.

In a few minutes, the great symbolic act was done. A half-hundred of the most important men in America had pledged their lives, their property, and their honor to the maintenance of the independence of these United States.

To protect them, or primarily their families scattered across the land, it was now agreed that the signatures would not be made public for six months. This was, at best, a dubious precaution. In a civil conflict like the American Revolution, supporters of both sides were scattered throughout the populace; both had accurate intelligence. Men everywhere knew who sat in Congress, and the great majority of the Signers had never made any bones about their American patriotism or their resistance to British demands. It was well known that the Declaration had been adopted unanimously by the United Colonies, and the British officials knew the names of the men who now represented the new states.

Whatever else the fifty-six signers of the Declaration of Independence did, by this supreme act of courage on August 2, 1776, they immediately changed the course of the Revolution. What had been a civil conflict of dubious outlines to some, now became a great national, patriotic war. This act drew sharp lines. When the Congress in July proclaimed freedom be declared in each of the *United States,* they had created not only a new name, but also the bedrock of a new nation, in being if not yet consolidated.

That this act made the Congress, and its members, legal, was not yet decided. Such questions rarely turned on legalisms. George III could not be voted out of office, nor could Parliamentary rule merely be declared unconstitutional. *Blows must decide,* or *powder and ball,* as Stephen Hopkins of Rhode Island put it, when Rhode Island seceded unilaterally in May, 1776.

All Americans know what became of the new nation these men declared and stood ready to support. But very few are aware of what happened to the men who signed the Declaration of Independence.

All these men, the few firebrands and the prudent ones alike, were conscious of their personal peril. As John Adams had written, *There is one ugly reflection. Brutus and Cassius were conquered and slain. Hampden died in the field,*

Sidney on the scaffold, Harrington in jail, etc. This is cold comfort. Politics is an ordeal path among red hot plowshares. Who, then, would be a politician for the pleasure of running barefoot among them? History was strewn with the bones and blood of freedom fighters, and the Signers knew it.

Their ordeals were about to begin. . . .

FOUR DELEGATES FROM NEW YORK

The Toil, and Blood, and

The delegates from New York signed the Declaration of Independence on August 2, 1776, with a British armada standing off Long Island. All of these men had a sober awareness that they might be signing away their worldly possessions as well as their families' safety, and their own freedom.

The Colony of New York, with Pennsylvania and New Jersey, had been the great melting pot of British America. The New England provinces and the Southern colonies were then almost entirely English in background, puritan in the North, "cavalier" or Anglican in the South, with a strong infusion of Scots-Irish Presbyterianism along the western Appalachian frontier from Pennsylvania to North Carolina. The three Middle Atlantic colonies, however, had been settled by a more diverse group: Dutch, Huguenots, Scots, Swedes, Germans, and Irish, in addition to the dominant English. By the middle of the eighteenth century these peoples—all heavily Protestant—had intermarried freely, with rapid Anglicization. The Dutch and the French Huguenots, as separate cultural groups, had virtually disappeared, especially in the higher echelons of colonial society. The amalgam of peoples and ethics made the town of New York distinctly mercantile and commercial, though the Dutch "patroon" system of extensive manors and large landholdings continued in the country up the Hudson. English-Scots business sense, Huguenot craftsmanship, and Dutch industry blended and created a new climate, where rich men built elegant manor houses and lived the life of English country squires, but also, believing deeply in the Dutch Reformed Church's ethic of hard work, attention to business, and moral, if not physical austerity, founded seminaries and libraries as well.

As in most of Colonial America, there was no sharp division between mercantile and landed wealth. Landed gentlemen invested in commerce, as in England, but they also actively worked at it, or sent their sons into counting houses, too. While the society of eighteenth-century New York is frequently described as aristocratic—and it was in comparison to much of New England—the upper classes there were more a working patriciate than a genuine aristocracy on the European scale. The colony prospered, and the society produced a remarkable group of men of affairs. Four of them represented New York in Philadelphia in August, 1776.

Phil. Livingston

The most prominent of the delegation was Philip Livingston, born in 1716. Livingston's grandfather, a political-religious Presbyterian émigré from Great Britain, had first gone to Holland, then had followed the path of the Pilgrims a half-century before Philip's birth. He settled in the Colony of New York, then a province newly-seized from the Dutch. He was able to secure a royal grant for 160,000 acres in the almost uncharted and totally undeveloped country up the Hudson River. Robert Livingston attacked this opportunity with energy, brought in settlers, and established the prosperous Manor of Livingston. He became a power in the colony—not always admired but too important to ignore—and his sons grew up to rank among the most respected men in the region.

Young Philip Livingston was thus "to the manor born." He came into the world with both wealth and high standing in New York. This position allowed him to enjoy the advantages of a "correspondent education"—he was tutored through the equivalent of grade school and college by post, and received a degree from Yale College in 1737. Yale had already become the favorite institution of higher learning for the gentry of New York, but as late as 1746, when Philip Livingston was thirty, there were still only 15 bona fide college graduates in the colony. Among this select group, which included Lieutenant-Governor James De-lancey and the William Smith who later became chief justice of Canada, were Philip and his three brothers.

Young Livingston entered commerce, importing and selling goods from England. He had capital and connections and he made an immense success. He married Christina Ten Broeck, from whose family name may have come "Brooklyn." He erected a fine country estate in the area that is now called Brooklyn Heights and built a large town house on Duke Street in the small but thriving town of New York. The colony in these years had approximately 100,000 inhabitants, and about 10,000 lived in the city.

One of the earliest biographers of Philip Livingston mentioned that, like most of his family, he *had virtues and ability as well as fortune.* This does seem to have been the case. In 1755, Admiral Sir Charles Hardy, the royal governor of the colony, said of him, *No one is more esteemed for energy, promptness, and public spirit.* Livingston used both his great prestige and growing fortune to benefit many public enterprises in New York. In 1754, he was one of the principal endowers of the New York City Library. He aided in the establishment of King's College, founded, as most colleges were then, to train clergy; this later became Columbia University. Livingston himself founded the New York Chamber of Commerce in the year 1770, and endowed the City Hospital one year later.

All accounts of Livingston show him as a dignified, austere man in his public social relations. Although there were important exceptions, this mode of conduct was so common to so many of the American gentry of the era that it seems to have been something of a standard. Washington, whom his close associates described as a man of intense charm, was cool and austere in public, leaving a lasting

27

public, rather than private, image behind. Livingston, likewise, was not easily approachable; he did not make friends easily, though he was described as a warm, genial, and friendly person to those within his circle.

Livingston also seemed to possess an intuitive grasp of the motives of men, a trait not only revealing of intelligence, but almost a necessity for a public figure of immense wealth and prestige. Livingston was rich enough to be disinterested in the affairs of most men, and to this he added perceptive intelligence of what other people were about. When he went into politics, as the custom of the time almost demanded, these traits gained him both respect and enmity.

Livingston was elected one of the seven aldermen of New York City in 1754, in voting which was open to all free citizens. He was also elected to the New York Provincial Assembly as one of the four representatives from the town.

The Assembly held 27 members, chosen from the City and County of New York, the City and County of Albany, the Borough of West Chester, the Township of Schenectady, the counties of Kings, Queens, Suffolk, Richmond, West Chester, Dutchess, Ulster, and Orange; there was also one delegate elected from each of the manors of Livingston, Cortlandt, and Rensselaerwyck. The manors were not mere estates, but genuine political subdivisions, with the rights and privileges of counties or towns. The "lord of the manor," under royal grant, exercised both political leadership and some judicial power. At the time Philip Livingston was elected to the Assembly from New York City, one of his brothers held a seat from the Manor in the north.

The New York colonial political system and power structure was roughly similar to those of most of the British provinces in America. The Assembly, home-grown and home-elected, did have the legal power to enact domestic legislation, though each act had to be ratified—or disallowed—by the King-in-Council, after the royal governor's signature. Its principal duty—and source of power—lay in raising money for public enterprises such as defense, officials' stipends, and roads.

The post of Assemblyman paid six shillings, five pence per day, hardly enough money even then to interest any man of affairs. However, it was obviously a place of considerable power, and in Colonial America, a place of great honor as well. The posts were vied for by members of the most prominent families, and there was considerable political and personal rivalry among some of them. The Delanceys, who were perhaps the premier New York family of the time, and the Livingstons and others carried on a kind of bloodless feud. At the period when Livingston joined the provincial assembly, local controversies and personal considerations clouded colonial politics. There had been little real trouble between "American" and "British" interests, outside of what had become a sort of normal tug of war between assemblies and governors everywhere. In the French and Indian War, men and money were raised by the Assembly. As throughout New England, these levies were voted willingly, though with a natural difference of opinion. Americans, generally, felt the colonies had done a fair share; the British Government, which did bear most of the burden, never agreed the colonies had done enough. This led directly to the Parliamentary plan to tax in 1763, but for some years the major fireworks in the New York Assembly were set off by power struggles among Livingstons, Delanceys, and others.

Philip Livingston became embroiled with James Delancey, who, in Governor Admiral Sir Charles Hardy's absence, actually administered the office from his lieutenant-governor's chair. In 1758, Delancey dissolved the Assembly because of these squabbles. The Lieutenant-Governor represented no particular ideology or party, and he was perhaps more typical of European politicians than the American gentry of the era. Power-hungry, dominated by personal and family interests, he seemed determined to establish personal ascendancy over the Assembly. He was somewhat typical—and unfortunately regarded by Americans as perfectly typical—of the kind of American who held Crown positions: arrogant, "in," arbitrary, and snobbish to a degree. His power and pretensions were deeply resented by the Livingstons. Delancey alienated a considerable number of prominent New Yorkers in these years, and while he had nothing to do with fomenting the Revolution or the British acts that led to it, he did have some effect on the eventual line-ups between "Whigs" and "Tories" in New York.

There was a sort of "in" and "out" factionalism among the Assemblymen long before the Stamp Act arrived. The "ins" were mostly those who for personal or business reasons felt they had to go along with the Administration, which meant the Delancey side. There was no division along class lines, for the Livingstons, Ten Broecks, Schuylers, and others were as much local grandees as the Delanceys. They, however, were the "outs," and made to know it through a lack of favor.

How much effect being an "out" had on Philip Livingston is not truly known, but the "outs" generally were disposed to oppose the Administration group when an actual issue arose. A large number of New York landowners and merchants, holding an enormous stake under the British flag, stubbornly remained Tory. But a significant number of the same kind of men did not. As a member of a great family holding a royal land grant, and as a wealthy merchant operating under British control of the seas, Livingston might have been expected to side with the Royalist clique which was dominant in New York City. He did not. He was one of those who took an "American" position, rather than an imperial one, from the first.

When Parliament, in 1763, passed its first acts indicating its intention to tighten regulation of the colonies, and to tax them, Livingston was firmly hostile. His chance to speak publicly came in 1764, when Royal Lieutenant-Governor Cadwallader Colden proposed to the Assembly that it pass a resolution accepting the Parliamentary decision. Livingston took the floor. This, he said, *"was alarming news from "home."*

Colden flushed with anger, but Livingston continued: *We hope Your Honor will join us in an endeavor to secure that great badge of English liberty, of being taxed only with our own consent, to which we conceive all His Majesty's subjects at home and abroad equally entitled to.*

The actual imposition of the Stamp Tax stirred up a tremendous, well-known ferment, not only in New York, but everywhere in America, especially Charleston and Boston. Even the less mercantile regions were badly disturbed. The Stamp Tax was not a piddling bite on a colonial economy such as America's; the duties hit some men and businesses hard, and they were fearfully looked upon as an opening wedge by propertied men less immediately affected. Unlike other Parliamentary acts controlling trade, the Stamp Act had a purely revenue character. It was imposed solely to

31

drain money from America. It put tradesmen and others immediately affected into the streets in protest and it opened up a frightening vista to educated Americans. They were even better grounded than Britishers in seventeenth-century English history, the period when most Americans' ancestors had fled to the New World. The great struggle for English liberties had centered around the sacred rights of the home and private property from invasion by arbitrary government; to Americans there was a direct link between the ship money extorted by the Stuarts and the Stamp Act. The whole constitutional problem centered around whether or not America and Great Britain were two separate countries, under a common Crown. If they were, then Parliament had no right to tax Americans under British law. If they were not, then Americans basically were British subjects without representation at the power center of the Empire, and taxing them could also be held unconstitutional. To lay the whole problem to *a sordid attachment to an inconsiderable sum of money*, as George Grenville did, showed a disastrous British misunderstanding of the people they were dealing with.

The Stamp Act caused riots in New York. Newspapers announced it in notices bordered in black and illustrated with death's heads. Associations were formed to resist it. Even the Royalist faction would not defend the tax specifically. The tax was self-defeating; it raised no revenue because it could not be enforced. The Grenville ministry fell—though not because of the tax—and the following Rockingham administration sensibly repealed it. This might have ended the matter, except that the clever Charles Townshend became Chancellor of the Exchequer in 1767. Townshend was determined to raise funds for his deficit in

America, and to do it through the Navigation Acts regulating trade. The new duties on glass, paper, pasteboard, paint, and tea kept the controversy alive. The newly-efficient enforcement of customs duties, on the inter-American trade that had never been really enforced before, was bound to precipitate crisis. In the decade after 1767, British revenue officers, aided by the Royal Navy, took £257,000 at colonial customs houses.

This tapping of the mercantile blood stream would have been resented in any case, but there were also side irritants. The King's officers were peculiarly arbitrary and arrogant with colonials on seizures. Americans accused of tax or duty evasion were remanded to special Admiralty courts, outside the regular judicial framework, which was supported by domestic taxation. The Admiralty courts conducted trials by Crown officers, whose pay came wholly from fines and forfeitures adjudged by themselves. The basic flaw was, or should have been, obvious; besides, this system abrogated a basic British right, trial by jury. The fact that no American jury would have returned verdicts for the Crown merely showed there was something wrong with the law.

Another side effect was that while £83,000 of the duties collected was remitted to London some £32,000 was used in America for civil lists. This offered the royal governors some freedom from their haggling legislatures. In Massachusetts Bay, Governor Thomas Hutchinson felt he could take a high hand with his assembly. The situation, though not quite so explosive as in New England, was analogous in New York.

The Assembly grew increasing resentful and refractory. The royal governors, whose offices were regarded as sinecures in Whitehall, and who were changed frequently, began to have a very rough time. The Assembly would not cooperate with governors who took positions of support for the ministry and Parliament. The governors, creatures of the ministry, could do nothing else. By 1768 there was a sort of deadlock in New York. The Assembly refused its consent to most gubernatorial propositions. In this resistance Livingston played a distinguished part; if he, and men like him, had not taken this stand, the impasse could not have been brought off; the Governor would have prevailed.

In disgust, Governor Sir Henry Moore exercised his power to dissolve the Assembly, hoping to get a less refractory one in the new election. The move backfired. The electorate was suffused with discontent, and returned an Assembly filled with men pledged to fight for American rights. Significantly, this new body contained some of the most distinguished names in the colony: George Clinton, Pierre van Cortlandt, Philip Schuyler, Charles De Witt, Abraham Ten Broeck, and Henry Wisner. This Assembly elected Philip Livingston its speaker, as a symbol of defiance at the very start.

The General Assembly opened correspondence with its colleagues in the other colonies, who had the same problems and shared the same sentiments. These committees of correspondence, in trading ideas, were greatly responsible for the quick spread of common resistance and moral indignation throughout British America. Nothing is more notable in the pre-Revolutionary period than the similarity of arguments, speeches, and remonstrances from colony to colony. The patriots in each colony were in personal communication, giving mutual aid and comfort. It was here that many leaders began to think seriously of America as one country. The establishment of communications among the colonies was a major political disaster for the ministry.

Sir Henry Moore realized he had stirred up a hornet's nest; his solution was to dissolve the new Assembly at the start of 1769. Now, the Royalist faction took the offensive. All the prestige of the Crown and the administration, and its patronage, went into securing a loyalist, or Tory, majority in the next legislature. The effort was successful. New York City and the surrounding counties returned 17 Tories to the Assembly. Philip Livingston was defeated for reëlection from New York.

Now, the great power of the Livingstons rather ironically worked in favor of revolution. Philip was sent back to the legislature from the family holdings, the Manor in upstate New York. Once again seated, he stood up and made his Whig, or American-party, views plain. He began to obstruct. And he was, as John Sanderson wrote, *marked for ministerial vengeance.*

The Tories tried to frighten him into silence. A Mr. Thomas, of the Governor's party, introduced a motion that Livingston be denied his seat on the grounds that he did not reside in his constituency, the Manor of Livingston.

George Clinton, of minority Whig faction, blocked a vote through parliamentary maneuver. Few Tories really wanted to push the issue; the rule that a representative had to live in his constituency was not British practice. Livingston was warned that the issue was dormant and future action depended on his own course in the Assembly.

Livingston's reply was an attempt to embarrass the administration by bringing forward a bill *to vacate the seat of any present or future member . . . who shall accept any post or place of honor, profit, or trust under the Crown, after his being elected a member to serve.* This was, of course, an indirect attack on the loyalist party; there was no direct way of mounting such an assault. Half of the Tory Assembly was on the administration's payroll or civil list in one way or another. The bill was vociferously voted down on a straight party line. The Governor's people were also infuriated, and Thomas' bill to unseat Livingston was immediately brought up.

In several days of debate, Livingston's friends insisted that the representatives of the people be independent of the Crown. The Tories fought back on the grounds that the Crown was not an enemy of the people, and Livingston's assumptions were anarchical and near-treason.

Although it was shown that Philip Livingston owned property in the Manor, and under New York law was entitled to vote in and represent it, and that for the fifty-three preceding years the Manor had been represented in the Assembly by a non-resident, and that, further, 21 of 24 members present actually did not reside in their constituencies, Livingston was unseated by a 17 to 6 vote. The balloting again followed party, or faction, lines.

The ouster of Livingston was the last significant act of the regularly constituted New York Assembly in the events leading up to the Revolution. From this time forward, the Tory majority dominated, and the Royalist clique in the city remained in control. However, if Tories were dominant in New York City, Whigs were ascendant in the rest of the colony. Their sentiment found an outlet in an assembly formed by Livingston and his associates. This "convention" was entirely extra-legal and had no powers, but it was hardly without influence. The quality of the men who joined the convention gave it standing, for these included some of the most eminent men in New York. It was this extra-legal convention which sent Livingston with a delegation to another extra-legal gathering in America, the First Continental Congress at Philadelphia in 1774.

The First Continental Congress grew out of the Committees of Correspondence. An actual meeting, face to face, of American representatives, was caused by the fulmination of crisis in New England, and the imposition by the ministry of the so-called Intolerable Acts: the dissolution of the Massachusetts legislature, the closing of the Port of Boston, and revival of a law from the time of Henry VIII, by which any American accused of treason could be shipped off to England for trial. Again, the British policy backfired. Strict measures against New England, in the early seventeen-seventies the most rebellious region, did not cow the other provinces. These drove them together in common cause. Everywhere it was said that if Boston could be closed and its population left to wither away or starve, the same thing could be done to any colony. The representatives of the several assemblies or legislatures met individually at Philadelphia to discuss the situation and to petition the King.

The First Congress was not for independence, certainly not for war. The main hope of men like Livingston was to restore friendly relations and mutual understanding with the old country. Loyalty to the Crown, as the concept of sovereignty, was very evident in the addresses this Congress sent to the King and to the British people.

The Congress met utter failure. The petitions were ignored; the Congress itself was regarded as rebellious if not treasonous, and the British Government, irritated at what it regarded as defiance, embarked upon a policy of using force. Troops were sent to occupy Boston and over-awe Massachusetts Bay. The next Continental Congress, the Second, was convened in 1775. It was elected in the colonies in the sound and fury at Lexington and Concord. Significantly, it was seeded with less cautious men.

New York, still represented in the Congress by the extra-legal convention, sent eleven men to Philadelphia, from the counties of Ulster, Suffolk, Orange, Dutchess, New York, King's, and West Chester. The group included Philip Livingston, Henry Wisner, Philip Schuyler, John Jay, James Duane, George Clinton, John Alsop, Lewis Morris, William Floyd, and Robert Livingston, Philip's brother. This was a glittering array of businessmen, landowners, and lawyers. Any five were empowered by the counties to act in concert with the other colonies for *the preservation and re-establishment of American rights and privileges.*

This was no mandate for independence. Most New Yorkers were acutely conscious of the value of the imperial connection, even while they were determined to fight for what they considered to be American rights. John Jay and James Duane, particularly, were vehemently opposed to breaking ties. Philip Livingston was dubious of *casting adrift.* While few men had battled harder against the British party by legal means, he was distrustful of the riotous Sons of Liberty, who took to the streets and were willing to resist force with force. He was fearful that the toppling of the Crown would only result, in the end, in *civil wars among ourselves,* as John Adams once wrote. There were elements and suggestions of social revolution or change in America in the mass violence that erupted in 1775, and Philip Livingston wanted no part of this.

38

As a member of a baronial family, Livingston found, or suspected, that his status aroused some suspicion among less-favored Americans. He was not overly-fond of New Englanders, although this feeling was not so much against the New England leadership as the riotous, democratic atmosphere engendered by the Revolution. Like a majority of the Congress, Livingston felt there was very little wrong with America, if only the British could be restrained. His suspicions about the Revolution resembled those he had held about Parliamentary taxation: a little democratization, like a little taxation, could be immensely dangerous as an opening wedge. He did not take a leading part in opposing independence in 1776, but neither was he a leader for it.

Lewis Morris

Lewis Morris, who was sent to the Second Continental Congress with Livingston, was, like the older man, to the manor born. The Morris family did not have the Livingstons' wealth, but they possessed even more distinction. The first Morris ancestor in America had been an officer in Oliver Cromwell's army; he had emigrated upon the Restoration. He brought some capital with him and was able to buy a tract of land near Harlem in West Chester County not far from the town of New York. He secured a further grant from the royal governor, and established an estate of 3,000 acres, called "Morrisania." This estate was entailed under New York provincial law with full manorial rights.

The descendents of this Richard Morris filled glittering

posts in America. One was chief justice of New York and later, royal governor of New Jersey. The three sons of this man became a judge of the vice-admiralty court of New York, chief justice of New Jersey, and lieutenant-governor of Pennsylvania. The family thus had more than purely provincial influence. Lewis Morris the Signer was the son of the admiralty justice, born at Morrisania in 1726.

Lewis Morris' brothers continued the family distinction in public service. Staats Morris rose to general officer in the King's army, became a member of the British Parliament, and married the dowager Duchess of Gordon. Richard Morris became chief justice of New York. Gouverneur Morris was to be a distinguished member of Congress. For many years, Lewis Morris appeared to be the least distinguished member of his family.

He received a gentleman's tutorial education at home, then entered Yale College at sixteen. Here he studied mathematics and languages under one of the famous professors of the day, Dr. Clap. He emerged with a Bachelor of Arts degree in 1746. Lewis Morris gave no indication of a taste for business or law; the family owned land, and he became a gentleman farmer in the environs of New York. There is no evidence that he became interested in the city, as Livingston did, or engaged in or supported similar intellectual or charitable pursuits. But he did become one of the first successful capitalist farmers, operating and improving his estate.

In these years an agricultural revolution was in full swing in England. New methods of farming were being introduced. English landowners were increasing crop yields enormously by an enlightened application of new techniques and personal supervision. Lewis Morris imported every new idea and application he heard of, and at Morrisania he showed a considerable surplus and profit. In addition to this, he married well, a prudent custom of the gentry. Mary Walton had two great attractions, according to contemporary accounts: she was *both amorous and possessed of a large fortune.* She bore him six sons and four daughters; large families were a custom among Americans of all stations.

During the twenty years that followed his graduation from Yale, Morris was among the most fortunate of men. Handsome, wealthy, every inch the American rural patrician, surrounded by a growing family and with close relations in high places in both British and provincial circles, he was an unlikely rebel. But he was caught up in the furor that erupted with the imposition of the Stamp Tax. He protested the tax, although it did not hit him, as a farmer, in any serious way, and he protested the closing of New York's newspapers by the governor, after they had printed news of the Stamp Act in the form of a death notice.

Americans of the Middle Atlantic Colonies gave illustrious descent a not-always-admitted admiration. When people like Lewis Morris, whose family was *greatly distinguished in the province* openly took up a popular cause, their political appeal was irresistible to the freeholders. This, in a basically free society, seemed to produce regularly a leadership of enlightened conservatives, inherently liberal in ideals, equally conservative in temperament. Lewis Morris, the squire of Morrisania, was one of a long line of American "revolutionaries," a line that could be traced to later gentry like the Roosevelts and Kennedys. Without, at first, any real reason to become embroiled,

Morris found himself elected to the Assembly, pledged to battle for the Whigs.

In 1767, supplies were requisitioned for the King's troops garrisoned at New York, the largest royal garrison in America. The governor demanded that the Assembly promptly raise the requisite funds. While the British soldiers were in America ostensibly for American protection, they were also there to enforce the King's law. This was understandably unpopular and raised a serious constitutional question: although the garrison was to "benefit" all the colonies, only New York, where they were stationed, was called upon to support them.

Lewis Morris was one of the majority of this Assembly who entered into stubborn opposition under Livingston's leadership. He publicly assailed the decree of the governor as *unconstitutional, tyrannical, and not to be borne.* This was one of the issues that led Sir Henry Moore to dismiss the group in 1768.

The defiance did nothing to prevent the levies, however. When the Assembly refused to vote taxes for salt, beer, and vinegar for the troops, the governor, using the "latent" powers of the Crown, simply requisitioned them. This produced a sullen silence in New York, but no acquiescence among men like Morris. He was so outspoken against the arbitrary acts of the Crown that in 1774 he was not chosen by the Whig convention to go to Philadelphia. He was considered too adamant and immoderate in his stand for American principle. The prevailing mood in 1774 was one of protest, but also of compromise.

Morris, however, was chosen for the Second Congress, as moods changed. There was one great difference in the new Congress. No one had yet come out for independence in 1775, but the Second Continental Congress was agreed that, if there were no concessions forthcoming, Americans had no choice but to prepare for war.

Some of the significant resolutions passed by the Second Congress in the early months read as follows:

That His Majesty's most faithful subjects in these colonies are reduced to a dangerous and critical situation, by the attempts of the British ministry to carry into execution, by force of arms, several unconstitutional and oppressive acts of the British parliament for laying taxes in America; to enforce the collection of these taxes, and for altering and changing the constitutions and internal policies of those colonies, in violation of the national and civil rights of the colonies. . . .

That measures be entered into for opening a negotiation, in order to accommodate the unhappy disputes subsisting between Great Britain and these colonies, and this be made a part of the petition to the king. . . .

That the militia of New York be armed and trained, and in constant readiness to act at a moment's warning. . . .

That it be recommended to the provincial convention at New York, to perservere . . . in preparing for their defence, as it is very uncertain whether the earnest endeavors of the Congress to accommodate the unhappy differences between Great Britain and the colonies, by conciliatory measures, will be successful.

Conciliatory measures and earnest endeavors failed. Lewis Morris was placed on the committee to survey the ammunition supply in the colonies, of which George Washington was chairman. The survey soon revealed that there was very little powder or shot in the public stores. There was some argument as to whether the report should be made public, or kept secret, in order not to inform the British of the destitution. The question became academic when Washington left Congress to command the Continental Army, and actual revolution in each of the colonies turned the arsenals and other supplies into American hands.

Fran! Lewis

The dean of the New York delegation to Congress was Francis Lewis, born the son of an Anglican clergyman in Wales. Lewis had been orphaned at the age of five. He was educated in the classics at the Westminster School in London, but quite early he showed he had no inclination for the ministry or any other scholarly pursuit. The aunt and uncle who cared for him placed him in a London counting house as an apprentice clerk.

Opportunity struck Lewis when he came into a small inheritance at the age of twenty-one. Described as *imaginative and romantic,* he immediately sold off his property and invested the proceeds in a cargo of merchandise. In 1735 he arrived, goods and all, at the Port of New York.

Here he met with severe disillusionment. Francis Lewis, with only a smattering of merchandising knowledge, had bought goods that sold well in London, but were too rich for the New York market. Lewis found himself stranded with a cargo he couldn't move.

Edward Annesley, a good-hearted New York merchant, met the frantic young trader and advised him to ship his goods on to Philadelphia, then far larger and more prosperous than New York. Annesley agreed to a partnership, and Lewis proceeded to the Delaware with his merchandise. He stayed in Philadelphia two years, and returned to New York with a reasonable profit.

Lewis now married Edward Annesley's daughter, Elizabeth, and settled down as a New York importer and shipper. Lewis had a penchant for the bold or unusual in trade. He shipped the first known cargo of American wheat back to Europe. He normally sailed with his own cargoes, and in an age when sea travel was quite dangerous, he visited every major port in Europe, and was twice shipwrecked off the coast of Ireland. He landed once in the Orkneys. He took a cargo to St. Petersburg, and voyaged through the Arctic to Archangel. So far as we know, he was the first American businessman ever to visit Russia.

In 1755, with the advent of the French and Indian War, Francis Lewis was appointed agent to supply the British forces in northern New York with uniforms and clothing. It was characteristic of the man that he went with the troops while on this business. He was at Oswego when the fort was captured by the French; reports said that during the fighting British officers were killed standing beside him. The French treated Lewis well in captivity, though he was shipped off to France, and not exchanged until the end of the war in 1763. On his return to New York, he was given a land grant of 5,000 acres in return for his services to the Crown.

Apparently he continued to live the life of a rich merchant. No thought of rebellion entered his head until the Stamp Act crisis. This Act infuriated Lewis. He became politically active; he joined the patriot group and enrolled in the Sons of Liberty, whose activist tactics Philip Livingston despised. He went as a New York delegate to the early conference among the colonies held during the Stamp Act furor of 1765. At this meeting, every colony had a representative except New Hampshire, North Carolina, and Virginia, and here Lewis voted for a resolution that proposed *the colonies be freed from all taxes not imposed by their own legislatures, and have the right of trial by jury.*

In 1771, Francis Lewis established his son of the same name in his business and retired to a country mansion on Long Island, called Whitestone. He continued to speak out for the American cause, however, and his reputation as a patriot caused him to be selected by the Whig convention of New York for the Continental Congress.

The fourth Signer from New York was a neighbor of Francis Lewis and, like Lewis and Morris, was of Welsh extraction. William Floyd's family had emigrated to Long Island late in the seventeenth century; they never proceeded farther west. By the time William was born in 1734, his grandfather had founded a sizable family estate.

Floyd's father died when he was still a boy, leaving him a fine landed property. The early accounts of William Floyd show him headstrong and not inclined to book learning. Freed from parental domination, and with the responsibility to manage his own affairs, he gave up formal schooling early. He was a passionate hunter, loving nothing more than to spend his days shooting. In those days, much of Long Island was a wilderness, with extensive native game.

Like many men of his unsophisticated nature, Floyd

was a generous host; he enjoyed entertaining the local island gentry at his estate, and riding with them over the
fields. In a day noted for lavish hospitality, he seems to
have been especially lavish. But Floyd was more than a
rich landowner who never grew up; by birth he was a
prominent member of New York society and he accepted
the responsibilities of the gentry. He stood for, and was
elected, assemblyman from Suffolk.

In the sessions of the General Assembly, Floyd enlarged
his acquaintance with the great men of the Colony. He
was notable, like Philip Livingston, for his distaste for
familiarity from people he did not know. It was said of
him that he chilled attempts by strangers to get to know
him. He was of middle height and rarely said much on the
floor. Again, like Livingston and many of the other gentry,
he was affable and warm in private. He impressed men
favorably; he seems to have won respect from both Morris
and Livingston. In politics, he showed himself utterly uninterested in abstract philosophy. His reasoning processes
tended to be logical, practical, and based on his own experience—the mark of an intelligent man with little theo-
retical education. Floyd took time to make up his mind on
an issue, but once he had, he rarely changed his view because of other men's arguments. Very early, he decided the
taxes and other measures of the British ministry were an
encroachment upon, even an usurpation of, American liberties. He entered the Assembly controversies on the Whig,
or patriot, side. He had many rich and fashionable friends
who tried to persuade him otherwise, but the squire from
Long Island refused to change his mind.

Floyd was typical of many American leaders from his
class, with the quality that made them such unique rebels.

47

Most revolutions begin in favor of some program, or with the burning desire to make change. Floyd had no desire for power, either for himself or his friends; he did not even want to throw the people he considered rascals out. What he wanted above all else was for the American colonies to be let alone—no taxes, no ministerial encroachments, no interference with the personal pursuit of life, liberty, and happiness. This was a view that pervaded the American gentry to some extent, though Floyd's was certainly more simplistic than Thomas Jefferson's. The dominant view in New York tended to be less liberal than the Virginian's, with less awareness that perhaps some of the gentry's liberties should be passed further down.

Because Floyd took a public stand against the governor and other Crown officers in New York Colony, he was selected for the First Continental Congress of 1774. In this gathering he failed to impress anyone by his oratory, splendid concepts, or the brilliancy of his fancy. He dealt in facts. He stayed aloof from the various American factions already building, and in his entire political career he was to be one of the few Congressional figures whose motives were never impugned, at home or anywhere else.

Floyd was perhaps typical of the men who made up the First Congress in his general moderation and conservatism. Samuel Adams and other firebrands were far-seeing, but they could have alienated the great middle-of-the-road American population of 1774. This Congress failed to gain what it had set out to do, win concessions, but it did accomplish three things: it called American attention to the controversies; it established the true points of conflict; and it strengthened the cause with a basically moderate people.

Floyd was elected to command the Suffolk County Militia when he returned from the First Congress. In this post, he drove off a British landing party trying to secure fresh water and provisions in Gardiner's Bay. This small fracas made him something of a Long Island hero, and he was returned to the Second Congress in 1775. He was one of four delegates who remained on hand when the crucial moment of the Revolution arrived in the summer of 1776.

The situation in New York was highly volatile at this time. Opinion was not so uniform as in other colonies. The Royalist faction was still strong in the city, and there was much Tory sentiment among small farmers up the Hudson. The majority sentiment in the counties was Whig, or patriot. Some of this political cleavage was over local issues. Some Tories were Tories because their party had been "in"; some small farmers were Tory because the great baronial landowners along the Hudson were Whig. Family and personal considerations played large parts. But provincial feeling, as a whole, trended toward rebellion against the Crown.

The Whigs never gained control of the regularly-constituted Assembly, as in other places. But the atmosphere became so explosive in the aftermath of the Boston battles that the regular government collapsed. The royal governor took refuge in a warship in New York harbor. The patriots formed a re-organized and reconstituted Provincial Congress at White Plains. This Congress finally approved the Declaration of Independence on July 9, 1776, pledging the New York patriots *at the risk of their lives and fortunes to join with the other colonies* in supporting it.

In August, when the Declaration was signed, only Livingston, Lewis, and Floyd were present. Lewis Morris, though still a member of Congress, was in New York,

where many of the province's patriots were serving in the
new local government or organizing defenses. The situation
did not stabilize itself. When General Washington, moving
from the British-evacuated Boston to repel the invasion
fleet expected down from Halifax, assembled his Continentals in New York, he found the town *alive with Tories.*
Governor William Tryon, from his offshore haven, waged
an intelligence and propaganda war, pledging an imminent return behind British bayonets. Washington was unable to prevent this communication between British ship
and Tory shore.

When the British flotilla was actually sighted off Sandy
Hook, great fear spread throughout the region.

Their families and property were very much in the New
York Signers' minds. Both Francis Lewis and William
Floyd had wives and homes on Long Island; Floyd had
small children. Morris, who signed after August 2, was
concerned but resolute in supporting the Declaration. His
own family and estate, at Bronk's Land, was within cannon shot of the British anchorage. But he said that although
he *felt and knew he was devoting his fine farm and mansion and valuable timber to the special vengeance of the
British commanders,* he had *motives of action in which
self-interest played no part.*

Livingston's business property and two great houses
were also within easy grasp of the invaders.

On August 27, 1776, the British General Sir William
Howe landed three divisions on Long Island. Washington's Continentals and the local militias defended bravely.
In a series of stunning defeats—though on more than one
occasion the untrained and poorly equipped American

forces performed well—Washington was driven off the Island, first back to Harlem Heights, then, finally, completely beyond New York City. In a few weeks, Washington was forced to retreat across the Hudson to New Jersey, with a suffering, dwindling army.

The invaders had generally excellent intelligence. They were aware, also, of the Declaration of Independence, as the journal of Ambrose Serle, Secretary to Admiral Lord Richard Howe, the naval commander, attests:

July 12, 1776. We also heard that the Congress had now announced the Colonies to be INDEPENDENT STATES, with several other articles of intelligence that proclaim the villainy and the madness of these deluded people.

Local Tories quickly informed the British which New Yorkers sat in Congress. Naturally, the American leaders were branded as traitors and ringleaders of rebellion against the lawful authority of the Crown. The resultant actions against them should not, except in a few flagrant cases, be considered as atrocities. The American people were engaged in war with the British Government, and in a bitter civil war with Loyalists at home. The events of the Revolutionary War were not unnatural in wars of that time, nor, for that matter, unusually cruel in the light of any war. The Signers were by no means the only ones to suffer. The path of war, with lootings, burnings, rape, and reprisal, cut a swath of destruction everywhere the armies passed. But the Signers, as premier rebels, were certainly singled out.

The first to suffer was Signer Francis Lewis, of Whitestone. A flying party of British Light Horse, under a Colonel Birteh, galloped to his magnificent country estate. Birteh expressed himself as very angry to find Lewis not at home, *so he could get the hanging he deserved.* The troopers vented their displeasure in other ways. Booted and spurred, they broke down the door of the mansion. They seized Mrs. Lewis, who was no longer young and had not tried to flee. The house was ransacked. Everything of value that could be lifted—silver, clocks, clothing, china, food, and drink—disappeared into British saddlebags. The furnishings that could not be carried away were systematically smashed.

All of Lewis' books and papers were piled in a heap and set afire.

The treatment of Elizabeth Annesley Lewis, as British historians admit, left a lasting stain on the honor of British arms. She was made to watch the destruction of her property and handled with brutality and contempt. She was carried off on a horse and locked up under guard in a filthy room. She was not permitted to have a bed, and for many weeks she had no change of clothes. The aging woman slept on the floor of her unheated prison, with only a slop bucket at her side. Under this treatment her health broke.

William Floyd's wife and children were luckier. Friends rode to warn them of the approach of armed Tories, out in force now that the British army was on Long Island. Mrs. Floyd gathered her family and fled across the countryside to the shore of Long Island Sound. Here, she found some loyal fishermen, who took the Floyds across to Connecticut, where, fortunately, they had friends.

On the island, William Floyd's estate was looted. The house was stripped of everything. The farm implements and livestock in his pastures were stolen; the extensive timberlands he had preserved were razed. After the house and grounds were looted, a party of British cavalry was quartered on the estate. Men and horses alike turned the house into a shambles.

The Morrises, like the Floyds, were able to evacuate Morrisania before the British redcoats arrived. The enemy decided to make an example of the manor as an object lesson to the rebellious gentry of New York. The manor house was looted and vandalized. The furnishings were destroyed. All the stock was taken for food by the army; the fences, put up at great labor and expense, were deliberately burned. All of Morris's servants and tenants were turned out and driven from their homes. Some of these poor people suffered greatly.

Lewis Morris had owned about 1,000 acres of fine woodlands in West Chester. These trees were cut down, and the land left littered with stumps.

Philip Livingston, the austere aristocrat who feared the Sons of Liberty, did not escape. Before the British landed, his lucrative mercantile business was already bankrupt. In 1774, Livingston had strongly supported the voluntary boycott of British imports, which was so effective that imports to the value of £437,937 at New York in 1774 dropped to only £1,228 in 1775. Now, in the fall of 1776, the occupation forces confiscated all Livingston's business property in the city. His two houses were sequestered by the Crown. The mansion on Duke Street was turned into a British barracks, and the estate on Brooklyn Heights was made into a Royal Navy hospital. The Livingston family fled to Kingston, New York. They had to flee again when the British attacked Kingston and burned the town.

The harsh treatment of Elizabeth Annesley Lewis by her British captors became generally known, and the subject was brought before the Continental Congress on November

8, 1776. Lewis' anguish was shared by his colleagues, who referred the matter to the Board of War on December 3. Washington learned the facts, and, by his personal intervention, was able to make a prisoner exchange: he traded the wives of the British paymaster-general and the Tory former attorney-general of New York, both of whom were in American hands, for Mrs. Lewis. Neither woman, behind American lines, had been mistreated.

After some months, Elizabeth Lewis was returned to her sixty-three-year-old husband. Her health was irreparably lost from the effects of imprisonment, and she died soon afterward.

Francis Lewis served on in the Congress, where his vast business experience was useful on several committees. The British occupied Long Island for the next seven years, until November, 1783. When Lewis finally saw Whitestone again, nothing was left but rubble; his house was burned to the ground. Lewis did not rebuild, but lived with the families of his sons until his death in 1802.

Floyd, all of whose estates were on Long Island, suffered deprivation of income for seven years. His wife and children were forced to live off the hospitality of friends. Hannah Jones Floyd never saw her home again; she died in exile in 1781. The loss of income, property, and homes by the patriots of the day worked a greater hardship than it might at first seem for men in public service. Not only did the men who expended their personal fortunes in the Revolutionary cause have no real knowledge they would be reimbursed, but most claims were not paid until Washington's Administration. The majority of all the Signers expended their personal funds to a remarkable degree in many ways.

Floyd stayed in Congress for a time, then, under the

Constitution of 1777, became first senator of New York. Contemporaries stated his example did much to keep the spirit of rebellion alive in southern New York during the long occupation. The influence of prominent men like Floyd can hardly be overestimated; their risks and sacrifices inspired similar actions from others. If all the leading gentry of New York had put property or prudence above patriotic principle, the Revolution could easily have taken a much different course.

When the fighting virtually ended after Yorktown in 1781, and some said the war was over, it was recorded that people of Suffolk County stubbornly insisted, *the war was not over until General Floyd returns.* He was not able to return until after the British departed.

His return was triumphant, with hundreds of people turning out to cheer him or shake his hand. He found his estate *despoiled of almost everything but the naked soil.*

However, Floyd remained prominent in state government, and he was able to recoup. He purchased lands in Oneida County, in western New York, and eventually moved there. Floyd's losses, though great, were only temporary.

The Lewis Morris family was also deprived of its manor and income. Morris soon left the Congress, turning his seat over to his half-brother Gouverneur, but he served through the war as a militia brigadier. He kept a small force in the field in the environs of New York. Three of Morris's sons also served as officers, all with distinction. In 1783, Morris found his property barely able to cover his private debts to British citizens, which he honored despite the war.

Dr. Benjamin Rush, a fellow Signer from Pennsylvania, wrote of Morris,

A chearful amiable man and a most disinterested pa-

*triot. . . . He suffered the loss of many thousand pounds
by the depredations of the British army upon his property
near New York without repining. Every attachment of his
heart yielded to his love of his country.*

Morris lived for some years in poverty, but he remained
prominent in public life and he was eventually able to restore Morrisania to its former magnificence.

The family of Philip Livingston was also kept away from
its home for long years. Livingston, now aged and ill with
dropsy, returned to Congress. In the next two years he sold
some of his remaining property in New York State to help
maintain the credit of the United States. He died, separated
from his family, in 1778; he never saw the property and
the mansions with marble fireplaces he had "signed away"
again.

Some men, as Lewis Morris wrote, have motives of action
in which self-interest plays no part.

THE JERSEYMEN

Through A

When General George Washington's little army, beaten in every battle around New York, straggled across New Jersey toward the Delaware, despair and anxiety gripped the surrounding countryside. The American Revolutionary cause approached its lowest ebb.

Washington had only about 3,000 men remaining. They lacked shoes, food, and blankets as winter approached. British intelligence, fed accurate reports by Tories, gave General Sir William Howe so much confidence that the Continental Army would collapse of deprivation that he did not pursue Washington hotly. Howe made no strenuous efforts to "bag the old fox," as the British called Washington, but was content to push him across the Delaware into Pennsylvania. The British forces then went into winter quarters in posts from Trenton to New York. The European concept of war, in those times, rarely envisioned winter campaigns. At any rate, Howe fully expected the Continentals to starve.

On the Pennsylvania side, General Washington himself approached the depths of despair. The enlistments of his *entire* Continental, or regular, army were due to expire at the end of 1776. Washington was far from sure that many would reenlist after his unbroken string of defeats. He wrote John Augustine Washington in secret, *I think the game is pretty near up. . . .*

As the military situation worsened, the American political situation turned darker, too. A certain amount of popular enthusiasm waned; many Americans who had enthusiastically supported the cause of independence in July cooled toward it in December. An understanding of what it would mean if the colonies, or newly-declared states, lost the war seeped in. In these months the British forces, with Hessian and Highland contingents, were brutal and arrogant; they cut a swath of destruction wherever they marched. Also, many latent Tories, who had been silent in the summer, now came forward. Loyalists in New York welcomed the British, and others in New Jersey now came out of hiding.

The new provincial government of New Jersey, that only a few months earlier had driven out the royal governor, dissolved when Howe's redcoats marched through the state. The principal political support for Washington in this crisis came from the Continental Congress in Philadelphia; and with his approval the Congress evacuated Philadelphia for Baltimore and greater safety. Meanwhile, in this hour of gloom, it was the turn of the Jersey Signers, those five patriots who had helped march New Jersey into the ranks of independence, to suffer.

John Hart

The Jersey Signers were a varied group of men, more representative of the whole population than the eminent gentry from New York. The delegation included patricians, but there were also sturdy settlers of middle-class stock.

The oldest of the New Jersey Signers was John Hart, of Hunterdon County. Hart was born in Connecticut, probably in 1711; his father, Edward Hart, moved to New Jersey when John Hart was about one year old. The elder Hart was known as a strong man, with a great sense of duty. In the French and Indian War he raised and supported a contingent of militia called the Jersey Blues. These men helped Wolfe's regulars take Quebec. He left his son a rather modest property and his own deep sense of responsibility.

John Hart was a farmer, and a very good one. He did not have much formal education, certainly nothing approaching the learning enjoyed by heirs of prominent, wealthy families. However, he apparently was well read in

certain aspects of English history; here his education par-
alleled George Washington's. By the year 1765 Hart was
farming 400 acres of prime land and operating mills at
Glen Moore and Rocky Hill. He was not really rich, but
one biographer states he was *the most considerable man
in his community.*

Hart was rough-hewn, fairly tall for the time, with dark
hair and light-colored eyes. He was called "Honest John
Hart" across West Jersey—the term had no cynical mean-
ing then. He was a devout Baptist, and he gave his struggling congregation substantial support by donating it
grounds and a churchyard.

Remarking once on his father's services to the Crown,
Hart stated he had no interest in wars or killing people.
His real interest was in his lands, mills, and enormous
family. His wife, the former Deborah Scudder, had given
him thirteen children.

With some reluctance, Hart was persuaded by his neighbors to serve in the colonial legislature in 1761. He was a
working farmer, not a gentleman possessed of overseers
and numerous tenants, and scarcely had the time to serve.
The Jersey Assembly in the middle of the century was generally progressive; it did much to lay out roads, build
bridges, found seminaries, and administer public justice.
The province was peaceful in comparison with others. It
was rapidly developing from a wilderness where wolves
still roamed, and, in 1765, it was regarded by the British
as one of the quietest, happiest, and most loyal of the
King's dominions. So John Hart served in the legislature,
without incident, until 1765.

In that year, when the Stamp Act furor swept America,
Hart spoke against the Act in the Assembly. He said he

61

would feel himself a slave if he were taxed, *to the value of a straw*, without representation. A man without public ambition, deeply devout, uninterested in anything but peace and continued prosperity, his immediate rallying to the American side at the beginning of controversy was significant. Men like Hart, in every colony, were an important part of the power structure, along with the lawyers, merchants,

Hart became known as a staunch supporter of popular rights. In New Jersey, as in most other colonies, collisions between the local legislatures and the royal governors became intense and frequent between 1765 and 1775. These collisions were the great nursery of the American Revolution, and they pushed Hart, otherwise a retiring man, to the front. The stripping of Massachusetts Bay of all its rights and privileges as a chartered colony, the suppression of its legislature, the landing of troops, and the promulgation of martial law through the Intolerable Acts of 1774, brought the resentment that was spreading throughout America to a peak. The colonial assemblies that remained unaffected by the acts understood clearly that their future was bound up with that of Massachusetts. The New Jersey Assembly sent John Hart to Philadelphia for the First Continental Congress of 1774, and reaffirmed his seat to the Second early in 1775.

Hart was one of the older members, but he took a very small part in the debates and maneuvers. He felt overshadowed by the brilliant lawyers and great landowners sitting with him; also, he was still operating his family farm and gristmills. He was forced to take a few months' leave from Philadelphia now and then. However, his reputation for honesty and straightforwardness was so great at home that he was again elected to the Congress in 1776.

Loyalism lingered late in New Jersey. However, the failure of the Congressional petitions to win any sympathetic response, the proclamation by the King in August, 1775, that all the Colonies were in rebellion, and the information that King George had recruited German mercenaries for use in America, at last pushed the Province past its Rubicon, as one of its legislators wrote John Adams on June 15, 1776.

The royal governor, William Franklin—the natural son of Benjamin Franklin—was overturned and expelled. Hart was elected speaker of the First New Jersey Assembly. New Jersey delegates to the Continental Congress opposed to independence were recalled. Four new delegates, all favorable toward independence, or at least not stubbornly opposed to it, were sent to Philadelphia: Richard Stockton, Abraham Clark, the Reverend Doctor John Witherspoon, and Francis Hopkinson. John Hart was again reaffirmed.

This delegation was authorized to join with the other colonies in declaring independence, though *always observing whatsoever plan of confederacy you enter into, the regulating of the internal police of this province to be reserved to the colonial legislature.* They arrived just before the fateful vote was taken, listened to a résumé of arguments by John Dickinson's "dilatory" group of moderates and John Adams' "violent" partisans, and then voted for the Declaration.

Richd Stockton (signature)

Hart's fellow signers included several of the most eminent men in New Jersey. One such was Richard Stockton, whose great-grandfather had settled the first patent of land, some 6,400 acres, surrounding the modern Borough of Princeton. His father, a sometime judge of Somerset County, had inherited "Morven," the family seat, and Richard Stockton had come into it in turn. Part of these lands were donated to the College of New Jersey, later called Princeton College, in 1756.

Stockton, born to a family of Presbyterian gentry, had received the finest education available in his province; he had then studied in Maryland, and in 1748 emerged with Princeton's first graduating class. He was a tall, fair, grey-eyed youth of fine speech, who made a good impression on his peers. He married Annis Boudinot, a lady of some literary talent, and studied law under the Honorable David Ogden, then the Province's leading barrister. He was admitted to the bar in 1752, and licensed counsellor four years later.

At the bar, Stockton proved he possessed ability as well as birth. Although few of his cases have been preserved, his services were soon desired by many who could afford the best legal talent, and was called into adjoining colonies. Working in Pennsylvania, he got to know the professional élite there, Philadelphia's John Dickinson and Benjamin Chew. He rose rapidly and made a great deal of money at law. When his father died, Richard Stockton was able to take up residence at Morven and maintain the mansion in baronial style. He had a taste for learning and the fine arts as well as law and he collected what many considered the finest private library in America. He also had an eye for horseflesh and bred some of the finest stock in Jersey.

It was recorded that Stockton was a decent and affable person; not the cut-and-thrust kind of legal opponent, but still one who exhibited great coolness under any kind of fire.

As his fame spread, he took other fledglings under his tutelage, which was a custom of the time. Doctors trained doctors, lawyers taught lawyers; this training was considered more important than special degrees. Several men who were later important lawyers trained under him: Elias Boudinot, who served in Congress; William Paterson, later a Supreme Court justice, and Governor Joseph Reed of Pennsylvania.

By 1766 Stockton had earned a considerable fortune. He was praised by Dr. John Rodgers, a fellow trustee of the College of New Jersey, as: . . . *A Gentn. of Genius & Learning, & you may assuredly depend upon his Intelligence as a Person of the strictest Probity. He is an eminent Lawyer & at the Head of his Profession in the Province of New Jersey. . . .*

At this time, he was requested to visit the famed Reverend Doctor John Witherspoon in Scotland; the trustees of the College hoped he could persuade that gentleman to accept an appointment as its president. The trustees of the College of New Jersey introduced Stockton by letter to the cleric in glowing terms: *A Gentleman of Fortune and Figure in his Profession of the Law, of distinguished Abilities, & Influence here, and a warm Friend to the interests of Religion and Learning.*

Stockton traveled the British Isles in 1766–1767, combining his mission to Scotland with a sort of Grand Tour. He was presented at court by a King's minister, and the Marquess of Rockingham, the pro-American Whig leader, introduced him to society. He visited William Pitt, now the Earl of Chatham, and presented an address from America, thanks for repealing the Stamp Act, to the King. On this tour Stockton frequently mentioned his belief that Americans would not consent to be taxed by a distant, foreign, Parliament. He was discouraged to find that this view, in the dominant British circles, was considered extraordinary. On this tour, he also visited courts of law and heard Sir William Blackstone and other great figures argue cases. He talked with Dr. Witherspoon, but was unable to persuade the Doctor's wife.

On his return to America, Stockton received new honors. He was named to the Royal Judiciary and Executive Council of New Jersey, which functioned as an upper house to the legislature and also advised the governor. Seats were filled by the Crown, and membership was a great honor. Then, in 1774, he reached the pinnacle of every true lawyer's ambition: he was appointed to the New Jersey Supreme Court. The appointment came just as the storm broke over Massachusetts Bay.

Stockton had never shown much love for public life. In 1764, in a letter to Joseph Reed he wrote: *The publick is generally unthankful, and I will never become a Servant of it, till I am convinced that by neglecting my own affairs I am doing more acceptable Service to God and Man.* However, with his career attainments, it was almost impossible for him to remain aloof in colonial America. His offices were not popular or elective; he had been appointed to high office by the royal party. Yet Stockton for some time had held a strengthening conviction: America's only tie to the

Empire was the Crown; it was outside the jurisdiction of Parliament.

This basic view—that America was another country—eventually influenced his choice, when every American in public life was forced to choose. In 1774 he wrote of an *obstinate, awful, and tremendous war* unless something was done by the Ministry. Because he supported American rights and pretensions, but did not desire full independence, Stockton must be classified as a moderate. His decision was painful.

He had success, wealth, social position, high honor, and power under the existing system. If he stood with what he believed right, the American cause, he stood the chance of being hanged. In the end, he opposed the royal governor and stood with the patriots. He split with every other member of the Royal Council in New Jersey but two, John Stevens and Lord Stirling. Stockton was one of the few "ins" who deliberately, on principle, sided with the "outs."

This stand had a strong effect in New Jersey. As elsewhere, the desertion of a considerable body of patricians from the royal to the patriot cause prevented the Revolution from dividing Americans along class lines. Stevens, William Alexander (who claimed the relapsed Earldom of Stirling), and Stockton, as well as Dr. Witherspoon, gave the rebels respectability beyond that engendered by honest farmers such as Hart.

In the Congress, on the eve of the momentous vote, Stockton had grave doubt of the feasibility of full independence. He was aware of the power, and also the benefits, of the imperial connection. He seems to have been finally persuaded by John Adams, who persuaded many.

While in Congress, Stockton missed election as governor of independent New Jersey by one vote. His supporters then rallied and secured him the Chief Justiceship. But Stockton, probably feeling he could be more effective in Congress, declined. He was put on the military committee, and with George Clymer of Pennsylvania he undertook an inspection tour of the Northern Army under General Philip Schuyler. He rode back from Albany and Saratoga just as the British army threatened his home state.

Jno Witherspoon

John Witherspoon, the big-nosed, big-chinned Scottish divine, through these last years was a close associate and friend of Stockton. Ironically, Stockton had not been able to persuade Mrs. Witherspoon to leave Scotland, but another American, young Dr. Benjamin Rush, who was to marry Stockton's daughter Julia, was more successful. Stockton and Rush had met in Great Britain, and Rush carried on the cause.

There were valid reasons why Dr. Witherspoon was so ardently desired in America. He had become one of the greatest figures in the Presbyterian world.

He was born near Edinburgh in 1723. Although this was frequently claimed by old biographers, he does not seem to have been descended from John Knox. However, he was a true disciple in many ways. He entered the University of Edinburgh at thirteen or fourteen. He earned his Master of Arts in 1739, at sixteen, and a divinity degree in 1743. Witherspoon was licensed to preach at the age of twenty-one, and ordained a Presbyterian minister at Beith, in west Scotland, at twenty-two. A few years later he was called as pastor to the flourishing congregation at Paisley, then a rich textile center. His ministry soon became famous throughout the Calvinist world of Western Europe and America, for his sermons and his published writings.

In these years the Church was split by a great controversy, between the Moderate or liberal wing, and the Popular, or orthodox group. These names require further identification to later ages. The Moderates, or liberals, were liberal primarily toward theology, diluting traditional Calvinism with humanism; but they also insisted upon ecclesiastical obedience in the name of improved organization of the Kirk. The orthodox, or Popular party, identified with the old-time religion and the right, so vehemently held in the seventeenth century, to personal conscience above authority, and the traditional right of the people to choose their own local clergy and to support no others. Witherspoon completely identified with the orthodox Popular wing. He became its greatest spokesman.

Witherspoon's beliefs were that dogma should never be sacrificed for what he considered at best a dubious humanism. He thought sermons should never be mere preachments of morality, and his were not. He attacked from the pulpit, with oratorical fire that listeners said could "chill" their blood, and also with enormous intellectual and moral weight. What he scored most often was the *spiritual vacillation of paganized Christian divines*; he was really declaring war against the increasingly comfortable ideas of a newer day that increasingly regretted the rigidities of the past. This, of course, was part of a recurring and endless battle not peculiar only to Presbyterians, and, in Scotland, Witherspoon was fighting for a losing cause. He also satirized his enemies—who were never so sure of themselves intellectually as he—with devastating, if not decisive, effect.

His last great doctrinal sermon was published in 1759, called *Trial of Religious Truth by its Moral Influence*. In it, he upheld all the orthodoxies of Calvinism, and thundered that religion that began to equivocate was comfortable, but dead. He painted a gloomy scene of religious decadence and the decline of stern morality in Scotland, and lashed out at the *insubstantial theory of virtue* by which a clergy too weak and intellectually dishonest to stand by the *great and operative views of the Gospel* was trying to win friends and influence people. He preached defiance, *no obedience*, to the ecclesiastical authorities of this *paganized Kirk*.

Although Witherspoon was honored by the University of St. Andrews with a doctorate in 1766, and received calls from pulpits in Holland, Ireland, and other places, he was presiding over a retreat. The Presbyterian controversy had spread to America, with the Old Side and New Side. The College of New Jersey was founded as a New Side or New Light seminary, but a number of influential people connected with the College had been deeply impressed with Witherspoon. The call to the College, founded at Elizabeth in 1746, moved to Newark and then to Princeton in 1756, came just as Witherspoon had outgrown his Scottish stage. He was forty-six, an advanced age then to emigrate to the wilds of America, but the College offered him a new opportunity to use his talents to the full. It was a platform from which he could influence not only New Jersey, with its large Scottish population, but all the Middle Colonies.

Witherspoon reached Princeton in August, 1768, to find Nassau Hall lit with candles in his honor, and important people from as far away as Philadelphia and New York assembled to greet him. His influence on American Presbyterianism was very great, because Witherspoon is given credit for uniting the Old and New Sides. In America, Witherspoon showed a vast pragmatic side to his nature. Whether he actually developed some of the ideas and trends that from his time colored American education, or merely articulated them, he stands as an enduring symbol of certain lasting traits in the American character.

As the sixth president of the College, Witherspoon found it a struggling institution, supported primarily by private funds. All American colleges of this period were founded as seminaries to train local clergy; there had long been a controversy in various American churches whether clergy should be locally trained, or imported from the surplus in the more intellectual centers of Europe. Although the founding of the College of New Jersey in 1746 was a triumph for home-grown clergy, on the arrival of the new President, in 1768, its funds and general prestige were in low estate. Witherspoon set out to change this immediately, with views and practices in education that were radical, for those times.

Witherspoon proved to be the perfect college president. He had erudition, reputation, and piety, all of which gave him standing, but he also possessed the knowledge of the world and insight into human character to put these to use. He was able to do two things: to enlarge the college from its very narrow denominational and theological limits and to win support and students from Virginia to Massachusetts. He augmented the college's funds and brought many young men of ability and character to Nassau Hall.

He changed the curriculum, which had been theological

and haphazard under his predecessors. He introduced philosophy, French, history, oratory. He insisted upon erudition in the English language, and a course called "policy." Witherspoon's insistence that the college prepare men for public life, not merely turn out divines and scholars, changed the nature of the institution. This shift in the wind permitted the college to turn out more young men fitted to shape an emerging America, and it was also imitated elsewhere. Witherspoon, a scholar, despised book learning for its own sake, since he found *many learned persons were greatly inferior to ignorant persons in clear, sound, common sense.* He denigrated acquisitive scholarship. To him, specialization in narrow fields caused narrow minds, crippled liberality and nobility, and made men lose their bearings in trivia. He had even less use for intellectual subtlety or imagery, and one biographer wrote, he *exterminated these* at Nassau Hall.

This great preacher, who sided with the common man's right to defy his clergy, who held to all purely religious orthodoxy, had a great streak of empiricism which probably was more influential in America than his religious views. A biographer claimed, rather sourly, that Witherspoon gave all America its doctrine of "common sense" being superior to acquired learning, *for whatever it is worth.* Whatever Witherspoon's responsibility, this doctrine did become dominant in American education.

The British-American controversy was already in swing when he arrived. By 1770, Witherspoon found students at the College demonstrating for the American cause. He himself took a clear-cut view, holding that logic and morality lay with Americans. His prophetic essay of 1774 showed the actual path the Continental Congresses followed. America would be loyal unless pressured into disloyalty; it would never submit to the authority of Parliament; it would prefer warfare to subordination. Although Witherspoon professed himself opposed to the clergy's being in politics, he found himself pushed into them, with the American party. His writings on America were widely read on both sides of the Atlantic, and he was elected to the New Jersey Convention in 1776. In politics, his lawyer and landowner colleagues found him a man of the world for all his morality; they were so pleased with his enduring patience and courage that he was sent to the Second Continental Congress on June 21, 1776.

At Philadelphia, he listened to the Dickinsonian argument that, while independence was advisable in the long run, it should be deferred until opinion in the Middle Colonies was "ripe" for it. He roared out in his broad Scots accent, *In my judgment, sir, we are not only ripe but rotting.* He voted firmly for the Declaration.

His *Thoughts on American Liberty* affected many of the educated gentry. Even during the worst of the troubles, Witherspoon reminded Americans that they were essentially a British nation, and the great values of British civilization should not be lost. He argued that the war was not a clash between two hostile cultures, but a result of British lack of understanding and liberality toward America. British institutions were not at fault. He opposed the emotional suggestion to abolish the English tongue in America and substitute German, which almost carried Congress. Witherspoon believed the cultural and commercial ties should be restored as soon as possible, under new terms, and this was the view that eventually, over much fervent opposition, carried in Washington's presidency.

Fra! Hopkinson

New Jersey sent another extremely talented man to Congress in June, 1776, in the person of Francis Hopkinson. Hopkinson, born in 1737, was the son of a judge of the Vice-Admiralty Court of New Jersey; his mother, Mary Johnson, was descended from a highly-placed English family.

Hopkinson studied at the Academy of Philadelphia, and secured the first diploma granted by the new College of Philadelphia, later the University of Pennsylvania. He entered the study of law under Benjamin Chew, then Attorney-General of Pennsylvania, and in 1761 was admitted to practice before the Supreme Court of that Province.

Hopkinson tried business and the law, and at this period in his life did not prosper at either. In 1766 he journeyed to England, hopeful of finding an official post through the patronage of Lord North, who was a relative by marriage. His connections, however, were unable to help. At this time, the only Americans who were being helped by appointments were those who had suffered from repeal of the Stamp Act.

Back in America, Hopkinson tried his hand as a dry goods merchant, then returned to law. He married well— Ann Borden, the daugher of Colonel Joseph Borden, the leading citizen of Bordentown, New Jersey. He rose quickly in the legal profession after 1768. By 1774, he was a member of the Governor's Council.

Hopkinson had both literary and musical talent. In the seventeen-fifties he published a number of poems in the

American Magazine, and in 1759 wrote his best-known song, "My Days have been so Wondrously Free," which was Thomas Parnell's "Love and Innocence" set to music. This is considered the first composition by a native American artist. He was active in the intellectual and philosophical activities and societies of the era and also painted.

Hopkinson, despite his Tory relatives in England, was an open Whig. He used his talents as a writer to pamphleteer and satirize the British party as the controversy deepened. In 1775, he prophesied that the colonies would declare independence. Hopkinson's talent was delicate and elegant, rather than hard-hitting, but his wit had a deep bite. A small, *pretty, curious, ingenious* man, as John Adams described him, his pen was credited for *irresistible influence* through its clever ridicule of the Tory and British side. These political writings were widely read, and resulted in his being chosen by the newly-dominant Whigs for the Congress in 1776. He voted unhesitatingly for independence.

Hopkinson's greatest service to the cause was through his pen. His best known work, "The Ballad of the Kegs," was written and published early in 1778, when the American inventor David Bushnell prepared a number of floating combustibles, or *infernals* and set them floating down the Delaware against shipping in the British-held harbor of Philadelphia. These devices, the first known floating mines, were constructed of kegs and filled with explosives, set to go off on contact with British hulls. Their appearance alarmed the British, who fired a great amount of ordnance and small arms into the river, at every floating object for some hours. The attack failed, but Hopkinson's satire on the British reaction was credited with being as valuable, at that gloomy time, as an American victory.

Gallants, attend, and hear a friend
  Trill forth harmonious ditty:
Strange things I'll tell, which late befell
  In Philadelphia city....

"These kegs, I'm told, the rebels hold,
  Packed up like pickled herring,
And they're come down t'attack the town
  In this new way of ferrying."

The soldier flew, the sailor too,
  And scared almost to death, sir,
Wore out their shoes to spread the news,
  And ran till out of breath, sir....

Sir William, he, snug as a flea,
  Lay all this time a snoring;
Nor dreamed of harm, as he lay warm
  In bed with Mrs. L.[oring].

Now in a fright, he starts upright,
  Awaked by such a clatter;
He rubs his eyes and boldly cries,
  "For God's sake, what's the matter?"...

"Therefore prepare for bloody war;
  These kegs must all be routed,
Or surely we despised shall be,
  And British courage doubted."...
The cannons roar from shore to shore,
  The small-arms loud did rattle;
Since wars began, I'm sure no man
  E'er saw so strange a battle....

76

The kegs, 'tis said, though strongly made
  Of rebel staves and hoops, sir,
Could not oppose their powerful foes,
  The conquering British troops, sir . . .

Such feats did they perform that day
  Against those wicked kegs, sir,
That years to come, if they get home,
  They'll make their boasts and brags, sir.

The last member of the New Jersey delegation has been described as a *leader of the dour, sensible American middle class.* Abraham Clark was born in 1720 at Elizabethtown, in modest circumstances. His father had been a town alderman, and left him a small farm. Clark was small and slender not equipped for heavy farming. He married Sarah Hatfield, fortunately for his career. His wife did not bring him money or influence, but she was a strong, capable woman who efficiently managed his small property, and thus allowed Abraham Clark to enter politics and associated fields.

He took up surveying, but his major reputation in his vicinity was as "the poor man's lawyer." Clark read law, but he does not seem ever to have been admitted to the bar. However, he gave valid and useful legal advice to farmers and people of modest means who could not afford regular legal fees, and was well thought of in the community.

Clark's personal views were strongly against the pretensions of the successful lawyers, who at this time were the most prestigious class of professionals in America. He boasted a desire to *tear off the ruffles from the lawyers' wrists,* and this was a view that then, as now, found much sympathy and support among the ordinary people bewildered and harassed by courts of law. His social attitudes were described as those of a seventeenth-century English "Leveller"—in other words, not inherently liberal, but strongly middle class.

His reputation with the public enabled him to be elected High Sheriff of Essex County, and Clerk of the Colonial Assembly at Perth Amboy. He strongly opposed the royal governor's party, and joined the Committee of Public Safety, which was formed to protect the colony against British oppression. This stand caused him to be selected for the Congress in 1776.

Clark was not brilliantly successful, but he had two traits that were widely respected: a hard-nosed industry— he worked at being a public servant—and a deep morality quite beyond the average of the times. He detested patronage and family favoritism, when both practices were part of the American way of life. Needless to say, Clark was more popular with the people than with the gentry, many of whom were lawyers.

In Congress Clark spoke out against pay for American military officers, against the printing of paper money as an expedient, and against lawyers in general. His firm grasp of morality made him enemies. He shared quarters in Philadelphia with John Hart and Dr. Witherspoon, neither of whom had relatives or connections in the city. From Congress he wrote a friend:

As to my Title—I know not yet whether it will be honourable or dishonourable, the issue of the War must Settle it—*Perhaps our Congress will be exalted on a high Gallows. . . . P.S. You'l please to Accept this on Plain Paper, our dignity don't afford Gilt, and our pay scarcely any.*

He voted for the Declaration, making the Jersey delegation's vote unanimous. And, making his famous remark about *Freedom or a Halter,* Clark was present to sign the Declaration in August.

The Signers were caught up in the track of destruction the British and Hessian troops cut across New Jersey in the fall of 1776. Each of them suffered severely in different ways. They were not the only Americans to suffer; in fact, the British at this period were rather indiscriminate with atrocities. Loyalists and those who had abstained from rebel activities were looted in Jersey in these weeks and months. But there was a special hue and cry after the Signers, all of whom were known.

Richard Stockton rode back to Morven just as Washington's defeated Continentals were streaming through Princeton, moving south. Stockton fed, clothed, and rested as many soldiers as he could, using up his personal supplies and stores. Then, as the rear guard marched out on the road for Trenton, Stockton decided to move his family to Monmouth County. This was thirty miles off the British axis of advance, and Stockton felt they would be safe. A good friend, John Covenhoven, took the Stocktons in.

But, as in New York, as the American soldiery retreated, armed bands of Royalists came out in force. A Tory sympathizer who recognized Stockton in Monmouth passed the word to a Loyalist band. These men rode off in pursuit.

The Covenhoven house was surrounded by these irregulars at night. The door was broken down, and Richard Stockton was seized in his bed. The Tories slapped the eminent Justice about roughly, stripped him, and took all his cash and his watch. Then, they threw him on a horse and dragged him off to Perth Amboy, now in the hands of the British. On December 1, 1776, Stockton was locked in the local felons' jail. He was held here for twenty-four hours without heat or food. By the time he was transferred to New York City, Stockton was ill; he had developed a cold which was turning into something worse.

At New York, the British officer in charge of prisoners made a decision that the Judge was not a political prisoner, but should be treated as a common criminal. Angry because he had no money to buy better treatment, the keeper refused to feed him for another day, then allowed him only the standard felon's fare in British prisons: a pound of bread per day.

Meanwhile, at Morven, British soldiery rampaged over the estate. It was agreed that since Stockton was guilty of treason, his property was fair game. His papers and library, the finest in America, were set afire. Servants were brutalized into revealing where the silver was hidden. Everything of value in the house was stolen. The furniture and clothing that could not be carted away was burned. Stockton's fine blooded horses were confiscated by the army as officers' mounts.

Dr. Witherspoon's country house, "Tusculum," was about a mile away. The British raided this residence, too, stripping it like Morven. Troops were billeted in the College, which then consisted of Nassau Hall, the largest building in the Colonies in 1756 when it was built. Witherspoon's prized library, three hundred books he had brought from the British Isles, was set afire. Because of Witherspoon's activities the College was considered a hotbed of treason, and the British officers were eager to stamp it out.

Witherspoon had been forced to close Nassau Hall in November, 1776, and classes were suspended for almost a year.

A Virginia Signer, Thomas Nelson, Jr., mentioned the damage wrought on Witherspoon's property and projects in a letter to Thomas Jefferson. *Old Weatherspoon has not escap't their fury. They have burnt his Library. It grieves him much that he has lost his controversial Tracts.* Two thousand volumes in all were destroyed or scattered, and the planetarium, or orrery, given by the Rittenhouses of Philadelphia was smashed.

The College of New Jersey was not to recover fully in Witherspoon's lifetime. After the war, he went back to the British Isles, seeking donations of new books to replace the ones destroyed, but met with little success. Witherspoon endured one ultimate tragedy because of the war: his son was killed in the Battle of Germantown in 1777.

Another party of Hessians, under Colonel Karl von Donop, marched into Bordentown. Here Francis Hopkinson had erected a beautiful house. The Hessians ransacked this, but did not burn it, probably thinking now of winter quarters.

As the advancing British neared the Trenton area, John Hart rode back to try to save his wife Deborah and their thirteen children. Hart was sixty-five years of age, a peaceful man, unwilling to fight or shed blood himself. He had signed the Declaration, somberly aware of the perils involved, because he felt it was right.

On the farm, Deborah Hart was dying. John Hart was unable to move her, and he refused to leave her side.

A flying party of Hessian *Jägers*—light infantry—approached the Hart place. They rounded up the stock and set Hart's gristmills afire. Friends begged Hart to leave; his dying wife asked him to escape. At the last moment, Hart ran for the woods. He barely avoided the soldiers as they surrounded the farm.

The Hessians and British secured dogs and hunted him through the hills. Mounted parties scoured the Sourland Mountains. Hart was considered an important prize. His capture would have a discouraging effect on the rebellious population. Hart was forced to continue running, hiding in the woods and caves, in the freezing December weather.

He could trust no one. Tories who caught sight of him gave the alarm, and he had several narrow escapes. Some cold nights he was able to sleep in patriotic American homes, but he dared not stay more than one night anywhere. Hart did not want to bring down punishment on anyone.

The British authorities offered him a public pardon if he would surrender, recant, and renew his allegiance to the Crown. The old man refused, and spent a frightful month as a fugitive. He was heartsick with worry about the family he had been forced to leave. By the end of December, New Jersey was firmly in the enemy grasp; the Hessians were making themselves comfortable in Trenton, and Hart was reduced to sleeping in the open, or in caves. No farmer dared take him in.

One bitter night John Hart crept into a large doghouse and huddled beside a friendly hound for warmth. The owner of the house refused him sanctuary, from fear of reprisal. Hart never complained. But afterward he described the dog as *a bed fellow in those evil times not the most exceptional, or the worst.*

Abraham Clark, also exiled from Elizabethtown in these weeks, was suffering a different kind of reprisal. Two of his sons—he had ten children—had been commissioned in the army, without his favor or patronage. Clark practiced what he preached about nepotism, a rare trait in the extended family of the eighteenth century, when society and government were loosely organized. Most Signers, like most Americans, believed family was the one thing a man could fall back on, in politics as well as business.

When Clark's officer sons were captured by the British, his values were put to a hard test.

The worst barbarities of the Revolution, on both sides, revolved around the treatment of prisoners. Neither side was prepared to handle large numbers of captives. Generally, the American side treated British regulars, and even foreign mercenaries well—though the same cannot be said of their treatment of native Tories. The British were at a disadvantage with prisoners. Although British arms passed over large areas, few places were safe or secure for the Crown. Prisoners could not be sent off to distant farms. The large numbers of American militia taken in the New York battles had to be penned up within the city. The British were masters of the spot only on which they stood, as Charles Carroll had prophesied.

In the early months of the British invasion, hideous things were permitted to happen, more through neglect than official policy, by the British authorities.

In New York thousands of prisoners were jammed together in cold and filthy sugar houses by the waterfront; others, for greater security, were taken to rotting prison hulks out in the harbor. Many prisoners of war arrived cold, hungry, or wounded from the battlefield. Their miserable condition was made infinitely worse because of the peculiarly vile type of individual who held positions of responsibility over them, such as Provost Martial William Conyngham (or Cunningham) and Joshua Loring, the Commissary. Loring made profits by cutting down on the food supposed to be fed the captives, while Conyngham, according to contemporary accounts, liked to stamp about the compounds shouting, *Kennel, ye sons of bitches, God damn ye, kennel!* He enjoyed floggings and doled them out freely.

The power of these keepers was supreme, and the high commanders, the brothers Howe, who were decent men, did not keep a rein on them. Disease broke out, starvation weakened prisoners, and many died. Old accounts claim as many as 11,000 died in New York and on the hellship *Jersey*, but this figure is certainly too high. The shores of Long Island Sound, however, were soon *white with human bones*, the remains of the dead who were thrown into the river. Probably, about 8,000 American soldiers died here.

Clark's sons were put on the *Jersey*. Because their father was a Signer, they were subjected to special brutality. Thomas Clark, a captain of artillery, was clapped into solitary, in a dark fo'c's'le hole, and went unfed. He managed to stay alive only because other prisoners pushed bread into him through the large keyhole.

Abraham Clark was informed by the British that his sons were on the *Jersey*, and that they would be released if he deserted the American cause. Over the dry dust of centuries, the anguish of this dour man can only be imagined. He refused. Further, he refused to bring the matter up before the Congress, or ask special attention or an exchange for his sons because of his position.

At this period, there was a strong danger that the Revolution would turn into a blood bath of mutual atrocities, because British arrogance and brutality was arousing a deep American anger. The British had not passed gently through New Jersey. In addition to the despoliation of the Signers, there were dozens of incidents in the wake of the armies. Francis Lord Rawdon found the plight of American girls in the path of the British Army very amusing: *a girl cannot step into the bushes to pluck a rose without running the most imminent risk of being ravished,* but the citizenry obviously did not share his attitude. Homes were looted or burned, women raped. American clergymen, other than Anglican or Presbyterian, were treated with contempt. One such pastor was bayoneted in Trenton. British cavalry hacked a dead American soldier to pieces. This mutilation was protested by General Washington, who sent the bloody remains to Sir George Osborne, a British officer. Osborne's reply that *he was no coroner,* and his refusal to condemn the act, caused merriment on the British staff, but cold rage among Americans. The foreign Hessians were especially feared and hated, but there do not appear to have been more atrocities on their part than from the British Grenadiers. Under the common assumption that Americans were rebels and *vile traitors,* as one officer wrote, no real effort was made to control the troops or observe the amenities of civilized warfare.

Now, two things happened. One was that there was a

certain change in the fortunes of war. The British commander in New Jersey, Charles Earl Cornwallis, made the mistake of despising his ragged enemy too much. He put the invading army into winter quarters at Trenton, Bordentown, and other sites, and took personal leave. Washington, with his army and his position fast eroding away, daringly took the offensive. On Christmas night, 1776, he crossed the Delaware and defeated and captured almost a thousand Hessians under Colonel Johann Rall at Trenton; a few days later he outwitted and outflanked Cornwallis and inflicted another defeat on the British at Princeton. These small actions changed the immediate course of the war. With Washington back on the Jersey side, at Morristown, the British evacuated almost the entire state.

Across the countryside, the British Army's repressive policies had not conquered the state, and above all, they had failed to seal the peace. With an unanimity it had not shown before, New Jersey rose to throw the invaders out. British troops—or Tories—were not safe anywhere, and the troops were pulled back to New York.

This retreat allowed the worn-out John Hart to come down from the icy hills. He went immediately to his farm. He found his wife dead and buried, and all of his children gone. His mills were burned, and his property despoiled.

Hart never found all of his family again; the children had been scattered by war and captivity. Worn out by hardship, anxiety, and final tragedy, Hart soon died. The Signer Benjamin Rush wrote of him, *A plain, honest, well-meaning Jersey farmer, with little education, but with good sense and virtue eno' to discover and pursue the true interests of his country.* Whatever the interests of his country were, Hart did not live to see them fulfilled, or to know whether his sacrifices had been in vain.

The second factor in tempering the worst brutalities of the war was that Congress, and George Washington, began to threaten retaliation. Word of Judge Richard Stockton's disgraceful treatment in New York reached Baltimore. On January 3, 1777, the Congress ordered Washington to investigate this case, and, if substantiated, *send a flag to Gen'l Howe in protest of this departure from human procedure . . . and know of General Howe whether he chooses this shall be the future rule for treating all such, on both sides. . . .*

The official flag and complaint brought the matter to Sir William Howe's attention. The Howes were Whigs, and while loyal to their own country, not unsympathetic to the Americans; Sir William had never been personally responsible for atrocities, in any case. The threat of retaliation, while salutary, probably was unnecessary. Richard Stockton was released, and allowed to return home.

It was too late, he tottered out of prison a broken man. His health was gone; he was never able to serve or work again.

His fortune was gone, too. Stockton, patriotically, had put all his silver and gold into Continental currency and bills of credit. This money inflated into worthlessness in 1777. With his rich estate in ruins, he now had to beg assistance from his neighbors, and put his family on friends' charity. A short time after his release, he died, at the age of fifty-one. His wife, who later wrote a pastoral praising Washington's capture of Cornwallis at Yorktown, spent many fruitless months and years trying to recover his scattered belongings and precious papers.

The Stockton family survived, and later furnished a number of distinguished citizens to the Republic, for one of whom the city of Stockton, California is named. The ancient family seat, Morven, became the official residence of the governors of New Jersey in 1951.

The news about the treatment of Abraham Clark's sons also reached Congress. Clark himself never brought it up or asked for help. But in a cold rage, the members ordered General Washington to take a British prisoner of war, a captain from an aristocratic family, and starve him to death in a dark hole.

Washington did not have to carry out this intemperate command. He found that a mere communication of it to General Howe was enough; the persecution of the Clark brothers promptly ceased. Apparently, some impression was made on the enemy high command, since from this time forward conditions of warfare in the Middle Colonies improved.

Abraham Clark continued in Congress for some time. He died shortly after the Constitution of the United States was ratified. None of his sons was ever prominent, and when Clark died, he had been largely forgotten by all except some of the ordinary folk of Elizabethtown. They could not afford a monument, but inscribed the following epitaph upon his gravestone:

> *He loved his Country,*
> *And adhered to her Cause,*
> *In the Darkest hours of her Struggles*
> *Against Oppression.*

THE PENNSYLVANIANS,
MARYLANDERS, AND THE
MEN OF DELAWARE

Maintain this Declaratic

ON December 18, 1776, General Washington held a thin
and apparently hopeless line along the western shore of
the Delaware River. He commanded only a few thousand
ragged, hungry colonials, some without shoes. The enlistments of the Continentals were almost up. Washington
himself was fearful that most of his men would opt out
of the war and go home.

It seemed that Tom Paine, who had given independence a mighty push with *Common Sense* almost a year
earlier, was writing in vain when he penned:

*These are the times that try men's souls. The summer
soldier and the sunshine patriot will, in this crisis, shrink
from the service of his country; but he that stands it now,
deserves the thanks of man and woman. Tyranny, like
Hell, is not easily conquered; yet we have this consolation
with us, that the harder the conflict, the more glorious the
triumph.*

Paine himself had already volunteered for service, with
General Nathanael Greene, when his essay, *The Crisis,*
appeared in the Philadelphia *Journal* in December, 1776.

Washington had these words read to each regiment of the Continental Line.

One of the great tales of history surrounds the turning of Washington's luck. His perserverance in holding his army together paid off, as it was to do again and again. The British failed to pursue across the Delaware, which they could have done, and went into snug winter quarters. The river remained unfrozen, and thus a barrier. The Pennsylvania militia turned out in force, to the strength of 2,000. Generals John Sullivan and Horatio Gates arrived with another 2,600 men from the north.

Washington's total strength climbed to about 7,500, just as the enemy chose to scatter his own numerically-superior forces in towns between Trenton and New York.

Meanwhile, in Philadelphia, although the Congress itself had vacated for Baltimore, certain civilians were working night and day to support Washington and keep the Continental cause alive.

Rob Morris

Pennsylvania, like New Jersey, had moved slowly and reluctantly toward independence. This province had its avowed Tories, too. But there were other factors. The large and influential Quaker group tended to remain neutral, or opposed the fighting on moral grounds. Philadelphia's 35,000 inhabitants lived largely off commerce, with and within the Empire. Her ships had sailed under the Union Jack. The war hit business hard. There were many merchants prepared reluctantly to accept a Crown victory, if it meant the early resumption of prosperity.

Robert Morris, the reluctant Whig, was not one of these.

Morris was another Signer born abroad, in Liverpool, in 1734. He joined his father, a tobacco merchant, in Philadelphia when he was thirteen. Two years later the elder Morris died, and Robert was left on his own. He secured a post in the Willing's firm of Philadelphia. Hard work, willingness to take risks, and a genuine flair for merchant banking soon made Morris a partner in the firm. He remained associated with Willing, Morris, & Company and its successor firms for almost forty years.

Morris' mercantile genius earned huge profits, which he reinvested in ships and goods to make more profits. He engaged in banking, money exchange, imports, exports, and shipping, the normal pursuits of a great mercantile house of that era. Willing, Morris, & Company grew into the preëminent business house in the Middle Atlantic colonies. Robert Morris was considered the merchant prince of Philadelphia. He owned an interest in two hundred ships and countless cargoes.

He also acquired a great reputation for integrity. Actually, no great merchant, in the days when banking and credit were largely handled through mercantile firms, could exist without reputation. Contracts involving men and houses in many widely separated countries were not enforceable in the eighteenth century. A merchant was only as good as his bond, and his bond had to be good if he expected to continue in business. Despite a pronounced bent for taking risks and thinking big, Morris had an enviable reputation among other merchants. He might squeeze a bit, but that was business. He never defaulted or broke his word.

The Stamp Act, that great catalyst of American resistance and politics, occasioned Morris' first appearance in public life. He signed the Nonimportation Agreement of November, 1765, becoming one of the merchants who agreed to import no goods from England until the Act was repealed. This abstention cost his firm heavily while it was in force, but it brought Morris into public notice as a patriot.

In 1769, now a wealthy man, Morris married Mary White, daughter of a prominent Maryland family. There were three sons and a daughter by the time of the final crisis. Morris was not really committed to active resistance to the Crown until after Lexington and Concord, but, soon afterward, he was elected to the Second Continental Congress of 1775. Morris and Thomas Willing, his less active partner, served on the secret committee for munitions, of which Morris became chairman. At the same time he was a member of the Pennsylvania Committee of Safety.

Pennsylvania was a proprietary colony, which had been dominated by its eastern financial and mercantile interests. Political control was exercised by the proprietary party of the Penn family, the important Quaker faction, and the Philadelphia gentry, who included a few old German families. The eastern oligarchy had held control of the Assembly through a systematic under-representation of the growing western counties, whose populations were heavily Scots-Irish and of recent, eighteenth-century, origin. The west was democratic in sentiment, and had real grievances with the east over frontier defense from the Indians, money issues, and representation. On the eve of the Revolution, the control of the old dominant families was slipping, and this internal revolution colored all events in the struggle with the British.

The eastern interests ranged lukewarm-to-hostile to the idea of independence. Pennsylvania was one of the colonies that took the lead in trying to find an accommodation with the British. Joseph Galloway's plan of union, which granted Parliament some authority over the colonies, narrowly failed in Congress, and John Dickinson was the principal advocate of the "dilatory system" of doing nothing precipitate or rash. The conservative element in Pennsylvania was not, on the whole, pro-British, but it was anti-war and hoped for reconciliation to the last. It was this spirit that made the Adamses despair that America would fight only *three-quarters of a war* against Great Britain.

Robert Morris represented this dilatory spirit. As his letters, especially one to Joseph Reed, show, he was not opposed to independence, but, in 1776, believed a declaration was untimely and overbold. He was among the majority in the Pennsylvania delegation to Congress that voted against Lee's independence motion in June, and again on July 1, 1776.

When it was apparent that a majority of the colonies

were going to adopt independence, Morris and John Dickinson deliberately absented themselves from the balloting. Among the Pennsylvanians, Benjamin Franklin, James Wilson, and John Morton were for the motion; Morris, Dickinson, Humphreys, and Morris' partner, Thomas Willing, were opposed. Their defection, on July 2, allowed Pennsylvania to join the other twelve, under the unit rule. Dickinson was not prepared to sign the Declaration, and resigned from Congress.

While the debates in Congress went on, the western democratic or "radical" element had seized control of the Pennsylvania government. This element stood for independence. Dickinson, Humphreys, and Willing were replaced in Congress on July 20 by supporters of independence; Morris, whose explanations of his stand were accepted, and whose loyalty was not questioned, was the only one of the old dilatory group returned. Significantly, Morris wrote that his original view was mistaken, and that an earlier stand for independence would have benefited his country. Although he had not voted for it, he signed the Declaration willingly.

His reëlection was fortunate, since he was to be a key figure in the war.

Pennsylvania legislators were embroiled in a running fight over a new state constitution. The one finally adopted in 1776 was highly controversial at the time: it gave the vote to every free citizen on the tax rolls over twenty-one, and created a unicameral legislature. This last provision contained the seeds of too much "mass democracy," unchecked by any higher deliberative body, for many leading men of the state. Morris, unlike many of the other Pennsylvania Signers, did not play much part in this controversy; he was too busy with specific tasks in Congress. When the Congress itself evacuated to Baltimore on December 12, 1776, Morris was placed in charge of its remaining affairs at Philadelphia.

He was authorized to borrow $10,000 to help strengthen the city's river defenses on the Delaware, and to carry on all "Continental business" while the main body was away.

Morris sent his own family to Maryland. He wrote afterward,

Having got my family and books removed to a place of safety, my mind is more at ease, and my time is now given up to the public, although I have many thousands pounds' worth of effects here without any prospect of saving them.

His first task was to supervise the removal of military stores of salt and clothing to Lancaster in the interior. He was continually opposed to the expedient of issuing paper money, which Congress had adopted to finance the war; even a few weeks after issue many people refused *openly and avowedly to receive it.* Those people who patriotically accepted or converted their savings into Continental currency suffered enormous losses, since this money was inconvertible, and the Congress, without power to tax, was soon without credit. There was, probably, no other expedient, since the opinion of the time preferred inflation to allowing government the only slightly more drastic power of confiscation. Paper money did have one great, unforeseen benefit: it forced the Revolutionary generation to pay for most expenses of the war, freeing the later Republic from insurmountable debts.

Robert Morris argued that the "evil" of vast issues of Continentals must be remedied, but probably no one, even Morris, realized how worthless this currency would become a few years later. By 1781, it took one thousand paper dollars to buy one Spanish silver dollar. Washington wrote that an army captain's pay for a year would not buy a pair of boots, and that a wagonload of currency would nowhere purchase a wagonload of provisions.

Robert Morris' enormous financial services to the Congress and Army are wellknown, but the background that made these services so important is not. The Colonies had a classic "colonial" economy, for the most part. They were engaged in both subsistence and capitalist farming. There was only limited manufacturing, mainly in the North. The surpluses of certain crops, mainly tobacco, were exported in exchange for finished European goods. The colonies did not have the means to make enough muskets, or even gunpowder, to support a single, sustained campaign. Such military stores had to be secured abroad.

Further, the economy and bullionist practices of Great Britain had prevented any real accumulation or circulation of specie in the colonies. The drain of gold and silver from America was one of the underlying irritants leading to the Revolution. What metallic money there was was not British; it consisted mainly of Spanish silver coins. The colonies issued colonial paper currency, and used sterling monies of account, but this paper was never at par with British sterling; it was always heavily discounted.

At the beginning of the conflict, hard money as always went underground. The separate colonies issued large amounts of paper, which they supported with different degrees of financial discipline. On top of this, to support a Continental Army, the Congress issued disastrous amounts of its own bills of credit—far more than it could hope to redeem. Under these conditions, with no powers of taxation, the Congress was never able to provide enough of anything—although noticeably the British invaders, who paid out gold, never had difficulty in buying supplies.

Although loans were secured from the French and other governments, these loans were primarily furnished in goods, not large amounts of specie. It was these conditions that made the support of individual men, and private credit, payable in real money, so vital during the war years. Again and again, Washington's fate hung on the supply of a few thousand dollars in silver, and while Morris performed feats of genius in balancing paper accounts, his, and other financiers' real service was in coming up with crucial, spendable cash.

The only real credit available to the Continental cause at times was the personal credit of its members. This was pledged freely, by men such as Livingston, Hancock, and Stockton; they took enormous losses, and for the most part, were never reimbursed. Interestingly enough, these continuing problems of money and credit led to the first Constitutional Convention in 1787, which grew out of a monetary conference called in 1785. The problem Washington and Hamilton attacked most vigorously in 1789 was that of sound money and national credit. Out of the lessons of the Revolution, the United States did not again issue inconvertible money as legal tender until the Civil War.

Washington could not have fought his New Jersey winter campaign without Morris. Morris secured the money that supplied the Army on the Delaware, and permitted Washington to capture Trenton. But four days later Washington made a desperate appeal to Morris again: he had to have more money to make good his promise of a bounty to the troops for six weeks' further service. Washington's appeals, plus the promise of support and pay, had kept half the army intact. Washington at this time had only some four hundred Spanish milled dollars, which were earmarked for the purpose of buying news of the British movements in New Jersey.

Morris wrote back, *I am up Very early this morning to despatch a supply of $50,000 to your Excellency . . . but it will not be got away so early as I could wish, for none concerned in this movement except myself are up. . . . you may depend on my exertions either in a public or private capacity.*

Morris' circle of friends and integrity allowed him to raise $50,000 in specie at this time. The story, which is neither provable nor disprovable, is that Morris approached a wealthy Quaker and asked for the money for Washington. The man hesitated. Only when Morris pledged his own personal note and honor was the money promptly tendered.

This money allowed Washington to win the victory at Princeton and free New Jersey from the invaders.

Afterward, Morris worked tirelessly, both in his private and public capacity to secure arms, ammunition, and military stores for the United States. His experience, connections, and *art*, as it was described, were invaluable. Morris took great risks, but he secured the vital stores without which Washington acknowledged he could not have stayed in the field. In these operations Morris worked closely with Benjamin Franklin, who understood equally well that the colonies could not support a war with their own resources. Morris and Franklin were making secret deals with the French even before the formal alliance was signed. Morris bought munitions from the Dutch, who were unwilling, out of fear of British reprisal, to let it be known. These were private, not government, deals so far as the foreign sellers were concerned. Without Morris' credit and experience they could scarcely have been made.

Out of these deals Morris did make great profits. His attitude was that he was entitled to profit: he used his personal resources and took huge financial risks. This was resented in some quarters on two grounds. He was allowed to trade and negotiate, in the Continental service, where other merchants were excluded by embargoes and other war restrictions. And his obvious wealth disturbed many less prosperous men.

However, while Morris did show an overall profit from his buying and selling, for the Army, he did take serious losses along the way. He lost some one hundred and fifty ships, and he spent a great deal of his original private funds. In 1777, he was apparently, with Richard Henry Lee and the brace of Adamses, one of the four most powerful men in Congress. He was offered the Presidency of Congress in October, when John Hancock resigned. He declined. John Adams wrote of him, *He has vast designs in the mercantile way . . . but he is an excellent member of our body.*

These designs led to charges of dishonesty and profiteering, supported by Tom Paine and others. Morris made no secret of his vast personal operations, or the fact that his personal credit, abroad, was far higher than that of the United States. Understandably, Morris' private and public accounts were at times confused. Congress investigated these charges early in 1779, and Morris was completely exonerated. John Jay, the President of Congress, wrote him a letter of appreciation. However, disapproval of Morris was strong among Paine and the "democratic" faction in Pennsylvania, and he was dropped from the state legislature.

Morris' later services, as Superintendent of Finance, are well known. Again, his *art* secured Washington the vital specie, as well as munitions, for the decisive Yorktown campaign. He badgered coin out of the French, and his books show heavy loans from Haym Salomon, the Jewish financier, who escaped from New York to Philadelphia. Morris accepted this final post only on the basis that he could hire his own people, keep his personal business, and dictate policy. Only the utter financial desperation of Congress made these terms acceptable. Morris was not universally popular, but his integrity, the personal honor that permitted him to borrow in the name of the United States over his personal note, was invaluable.

Morris did merit the respect and friendship of the important men of his time. Washington wrote that he owed no one individual more. Ironically, Morris became bankrupt and was sent to debtors' prison during Washington's Administration. He had taken one final risk on the eve of the Napoleonic Wars, speculating in western lands. He lost everything, including his home, but he had one consolation before he was released under the first national bankruptcy act: George Washington came to dine with him in jail.

Robert Morris died a poor man, in 1806.

Benj. Franklin

Robert Morris' principal co-worker in securing foreign aid and supplies was Benjamin Franklin. Franklin, born in 1706, was the oldest man in Congress, and at the time the Declaration was signed, he was unquestionably the best known American in the world. With Jefferson, he was one of the two men of genuine genius at Philadelphia. Scientist, philosopher, humanist, political figure, statesman, moralist, and author, he was strong for independence. He had been working for a union of the colonies—though under the Crown—since the seventeen-fifties. His appearance before the House of Commons in 1766 was credited with the repeal of the Stamp Act at that time. He sacrificed the office of deputy postmaster-general of the Colonies because of his American views in 1774. The successes of his long and active life, and his invaluable diplomatic services to the Congress during the war, are all well-known. He rose, as he said, from indentured printer's apprentice to stand before kings, five kings in all.

Franklin was also one of those who pledged his own property in the Revolution. As the controversy developed, he was told by a member of Parliament to remember *the exposed condition of the colonies, the power of England, the multitude of her ships, and the omnipotence of her armies*, which would ravage the whole coast and lay the seaports in ashes.

Franklin replied that this could well happen, but *though the chief part of his little property* lay in such towns, *the fear of losing it would not alter his decision*. Nor did it.

Franklin suffered one great personal unhappiness because of the Revolution. His natural—and only—son, William, Royal Governor of New Jersey, adhered to the Crown and died in England.

John Morton

The two other original members of the Pennsylvania delegation who voted for independence on that historic July 2, 1776, were James Wilson and John Morton. Morton was of Swedish descent; his great-grandfather had emigrated from Scandinavia about 1654. He was born in Chester (later Delaware) County in 1724.

Though early arrivals, the Mortons did not prosper greatly in the New World. John Morton's father died when he was very young, leaving the family very poor. Morton's mother remarried. Morton's stepfather was a surveyor, and the young man took up this profession.

In these decades new lands were being laid out in Pennsylvania, and Morton found his work profitable. He was considered a man of good common sense and firm convictions in his community. In time, he was selected to be a Justice of the Peace, a position of much greater prestige and authority than now, and a post most often held by the gentry. From this first public service, Morton rose steadily, until he was appointed an associate justice of the Pennsylvania Supreme Court. In his time, judges, even on high tribunals, frequently were not lawyers.

As a Crown officer, living in a section of the colony that remained strongly Loyalist, Morton felt pulled toward moderation in the revolutionary controversy. Most of his life, and all his honors, stemmed from support of the legitimate authority and the law. It was understandably harder for this man, who had worked his way up through the ranks of public service, to become a rebel than for some independently wealthy men who entered politics only when pulled in by the ideological and territorial quarrel. Ironically, he was one of those originally sent to the Second Continental Congress to express opposition to independence. However, he was also Speaker of the reorganized Pennsylvania Assembly which changed the delegation's instruction in June. A man of deep religious feeling, Morton seems to have had an enormous struggle with his conscience. He only changed his vote to favor independence on July 1, 1776, thus creating the deadlock which Dickinson's and Morris' abstentions broke. Once committed, Morton sustained the decision and signed the Declaration willingly.

The people who had sent him to Congress considered that he had betrayed his trust. Most of Judge Morton's associates, and even some of his family, were Tories. Whatever the feeling in Philadelphia in the euphoric aftermath of the ringing of the Liberty Bell, Morton's close friends did not forgive him. When Morton returned to his home after signing, he found himself ostracized by his former friends.

Morton was a sensitive, troubled, conscientious man. He was deeply hurt by the reaction of his friends. Contemporary accounts state that his rejection by the people he knew and loved best now hastened the failure of his health, and his death. He fell sick early in 1777. Former associates and relatives stayed away; he was made to feel he had betrayed King and Country, and he died almost alone.

On his deathbed Morton spoke out. His mind, in its last clear moments, was on the missing friends and loved ones. *Tell them,* he said, *Tell them that they will live to see the hour when they shall acknowledge it* [the Signing] *to have been the most glorious service that I ever rendered to my country.*

He was the first Signer to die.

James Wilson

James Wilson, who had stood with Franklin for independence as the final arguments ensued, was born in Scotland in 1742. His father was a yeoman farmer of modest means; however, he secured for his son the best education that could be had. Young Wilson attended the Universities of Glasgow and Edinburgh.

Realizing that as a young man of humble birth and no prospects of wealth his future was limited in Great Britain despite his fine education, young Wilson emigrated to America at the age of twenty-one. He stopped first at New York, then arrived in Philadelphia, in 1766. He got a job as tutor in Latin, and came to the attention of the Episcopal bishop, who helped him secure a position in John Dickinson's office, reading law. Within two years, Dickinson sponsored him at the bar.

John Dickinson, Benjamin Chew, and a few others had made Philadelphia noted throughout the colonies for its legal talent—a reputation that is still, a little pejoratively, remembered in the term, "Philadelphia lawyer." James Wilson had to cut a niche for himself against formidable opposition.

In his first case, Wilson came up against Benjamin Chew, then the attorney-general of the colony. The young Scot slashed Mr. Chew's case to pieces at the bar, and forced the Proprietors of Pennsylvania to settle with his client, a well-known land speculator. Chew, rather than being angry, was impressed, as was another eminent barrister present, Joseph Reed, who later became governor of the state. This success brought Wilson immediate business, and the established laywers gracefully made room for a rising talent. For a time he enjoyed a good practice among the German farmers in the Reading area.

Seeking greater opportunity in newer regions, Wilson moved to the Scots-Irish-settled counties around Carlisle. It was noted that by 1774 he was carrying one-half of all legal cases in his county and also cases in seven others. He became established, bought land, a house, a Negro slave, and married a girl he had had his eye on for some time, Rachel Bird.

The western counties were the seedbed of the newer, democratic sentiment in Pennsylvania. Wilson was an instinctive conservative, but also an intellectual republican. It was the latter views, more than his feelings, that brought him to prominence in politics. Yet Wilson was moderate, hesitant, and much afraid of returning society to a state of nature, as he said. Throughout his life, his own concept of democracy was primarily intellectual, rather than popular. Like John Adams, he believed sovereignty lay in the people but was highly dubious of the people's ability to exercise it. He did, however, almost from the moment he arrived in America, take the American side against Parliament and Crown.

As a successful lawyer, he was elected to the Assembly and became well known throughout the Colony. He was one of the first men to conclude and say publicly that the

British Parliament had no inherent powers to rule America. In 1770 he wrote, *All the different members of the British empire are distinct states, Independent of each other, but connected together under the same sovereign.* Thus he was one of the first supporters of the concept of the British Commonwealth of nations—a concept the British themselves then rejected. His pamphlet expounding this idea, published in 1774, had a strong influence on the First Continental Congress.

In January, 1775, Wilson became a delegate to the Provincial Convention. He introduced a resolution condemning the Boston Port Act as unconstitutional. This was one of the first public statements expressing the opinion that an act of Parliament could be unconstitutional— a concept that was not possible under English law. This, like his views on commonwealth, were prophetic; Wilson was one of the fathers of the distinctive American doctrine of judicial review of legislative acts. The resolution failed, but the idea remained.

Although in the Second Congress, to which he was appointed in May, 1775, with Franklin and Willing, he was at first a strong moderate, he changed his mind when the new Pennsylvania Assembly withdrew the former injunction against independence. He switched his position again on July 1, 1776.

Wilson was appointed as a commissioner of Indian affairs by Congress for the Middle Department, which included Pennsylvania. On this commission he showed himself to have moderate and peaceable views toward the Indians, whom his former backwoods neighbors frankly despised as vermin.

From 1776 onward, Wilson seems to have grown more

conservative in his viewpoints, at least toward the practical implementation of democracy. Like almost all Pennsylvania lawyers, he disapproved of the state constitution of 1776. This brought him into bitter conflict with Paine, the democratic faction, and the western frontier groups, and caused him to be dropped from the Congress in September, 1777. He continued to be caught up in local political squabbles. In 1779, a mob, especially outraged because Wilson dared to defend Tory clients at law, besieged Wilson and some friends in his house on Walnut Street in Philadelphia. He was rescued by the First City Troop, but had to leave the city for a time. Political controversy in his home state kept Wilson from national service during most of the Revolution; he only returned to Congress when the Pennsylvania pendulum swung late in the war.

His greatest services were to be in founding the new Republic, and in changing the Pennsylvania Constitution of 1776. Wilson, although he never became a symbol of a certain school of thought, like Hamilton or Jefferson, was extremely influential in the adoption of the United States Constitution of 1789. He wrote the draft in 1787, with the assistance of Gouverneur Morris, brother of the Signer. In this document, Wilson embodied his beliefs that sovereignty did come from the inherent rights of the people, but that checks and safeguards to their free exercise of it must be maintained. He was highly influential in forging a representative, rather than a direct, democracy for the United States.

He was politically vindicated in Pennsylvania in 1789–1790, when he wrote the constitution that replaced the controversial document of 1776. In 1798, Wilson died while a Justice of the Supreme Court of the United States.

Benjamin Rush

Of the five new delegates sent by Pennsylvania to the Congress on July 20, 1776, Benjamin Rush, George Clymer, George Ross, James Smith, and George Taylor, Doctor Rush was the best-known.

Rush was born near Philadelphia in 1745. His family were old settlers; his great-grandfather had been a captain of horse under Oliver Cromwell, emigrating on the Lord Protector's death in 1658. They were farmers, and described in contemporary accounts as *yeoman stock*. Rush's father died when he was six, but his mother was able to give him an outstanding education. He attended the Nottingham School in Maryland, which was directed by a relative, then entered the College of New Jersey at Princeton at the age of fourteen. He graduated at sixteen, according to the custom, with a Bachelor of Arts degree. Rush immediately took up medicine. Like law, formal training in medicine was more a matter of apprenticeship than study, and Rush worked for a time under a licensed doctor. Then, to improve his education, he journeyed to Edinburgh, Scotland, which was becoming the leading medical center of the world. After two years of study there, he was awarded the degree of Doctor of Medicine. The most significant event of Rush's foreign study was his helping Richard Stockton persuade Dr. Witherspoon to accept the presidency of the College of New Jersey. His efforts succeeded with the reluctant Mrs. Witherspoon where Stockton's had not.

After Edinburgh, Rush traveled through England and France, attending medical lectures and visiting the more famous hospitals. In 1769 he was back in Philadelphia, fortified with the latest European arts in medicine. Rush was a slender, animated man with blue eyes, *ambitious of the manners of a gentleman*, but despite his social graces and his education, he does not seem to have been embraced immediately by the Philadelphia gentry, or the more conservative older doctors such as Shippen, Bond, and Kuhn. Rush's early practice was almost entirely among the poor, although it was said that within five years he enjoyed a high income.

Rush was a practicer of the "New System" of medicine; unfortunately, like the older system, the new one was more a rationalization than a science. While many of his theories, by modern medical standards, were absurd, they were no more nonsensical, usually less so, than standard practices of the era. Rush tried to hammer everything into one rational system—an eighteenth-century characteristic, not limited to medicine, but also evident in philosophy and government, too. Rush's own comment about himself—*he aimed well*—is disputed by no one, though he was a highly controversial medical man in his own day.

Importantly, Rush's early practice, his origins, his deep religious impressions—he never doubted *the divine origin of the Bible* as he said—and natural instincts made him one of the earliest humanitarians in America. His fame was to survive for this more than his practice or discoveries. Rush developed a sincere belief in social reforms to benefit the sick and poor, at a time when the poor and sick were hideously neglected by society. He had a natural horror of capital punishment, and strongly opposed many of the highly brutal penal codes of the time. He was an early abolitionist. Rush was really a better writer, teacher, and lecturer than he was a practicing physician, and his fame rests more upon his publications and appearances than his medicine. He wrote sketches of the Signers, essays on health, slavery, temperance, and newspaper articles favoring the American cause—. . . *No form of government can be rational but that which is derived from the Suffrages of the people who are the subjects of it.* His writings made him the most famous doctor in America in his time.

These writings also brought him to the attention of John Dickinson, James Wilson, Charles Thomson, and other Pennsylvania patriots, and eased him into politics.

As a pamphleteer, Rush claimed that the *first gun that was fired at an American cut the cord that tied the two countries together.* This attitude, after Lexington and Concord, and his genuine democratic sympathies, led him to be appointed to the Congress by the dominant faction in 1776. His preparation of the public mind for independence was his major political service, although he did innoculate Patrick Henry for the smallpox. Rush encouraged Tom Paine, and picked the title for *Common Sense.*

Rush knew most of the Congressmen and Signers; his descriptions of them are considered reasonable and fairly accurate. Of Rush himself, John Adams wrote:

He is an elegant, ingenious body, a sprightly, pretty fellow. He is a Republican . . . but Rush, I think, is too much of a talker to be a deep thinker; elegant, not great.

Great he may not have been, but he was intensely human.

As a graduate of the College of New Jersey, an admirer of Dr. Witherspoon, and a friend of Richard Stockton, Rush became impressed with Stockton's oldest daughter, Julia. They were married in January, 1776.

Rush gave up his practice and his chair of medicine at the University of Pennsylvania and joined the local militia as a surgeon when the British swarmed down New Jersey later that year. With Joseph Reed, then a colonel of militia, he visited Washington's headquarters the day before the historic crossing of the Delaware. During this visit, Rush noticed Washington scrawling "Victory or Death" on a piece of paper, but did not know what the commander-in-chief had in mind. On Christmas night, the doctor actually took part in General John Cadwalader's unsuccessful effort to cross the river to the south at Bordentown in support of Washington's main effort.

In the next few days he was with Washington, and took an active part in the councils that led to the victory at Princeton.

But Rush meanwhile, along with many important Pennsylvanians, had attacked the new Pennsylvania Constitution and its unicameral legislature. This undermined his popularity among the dominant faction, and he was dropped from Congress by the Assembly in February, 1777. He accepted a commission as surgeon-general of the Middle Department of the Continental Army in April.

The campaign of 1776 had ended in a sort of stalemate. The British held New York and environs, but they had been driven out of New Jersey and blocked in upstate New York, near the Canada border. The British now planned a new offensive with a double object: to split New England from the other colonies by a march down New York from Canada, and to strike a blow at the heart of rebellion by seizing Philadelphia. The British, who always seemed on the brink of military victory but were usually dilatory, disastrously failed to coordinate this strategy. The result was, that while General John Burgoyne started south from Canada with a large force, Sir William Howe, at New York, took ship for Chesapeake Bay with the main British army. History might have been drastically altered had Howe marched up the Hudson to meet Burgoyne.

Washington, who tenaciously kept the Continentals in the field, marched to Pennsylvania to resist Howe's advance. He gave battle at Brandywine and Germantown, and although the Americans fought well, and the battles could have gone either way, Washington was sharply defeated again. He had to draw back, leaving Howe to occupy Philadelphia on September 27, 1777. The Congress again moved to Baltimore.

Rush was with the army at Brandywine, performing surgery on the wounded. He was almost captured after the battle, and escaped only by fleeing through the woods. His family was also in danger. Julia Stockton Rush was several months pregnant, but Rush bundled her off to a relative's home in Maryland; Rush's first child was born as a refugee. He also moved his furniture to a friend's house, but this dwelling was taken over by the enemy. General Howe used one of Rush's mahogany tables to write his dispatches and spilled ink over it. This was an "atrocity" of which Rush afterward was rather proud.

The invasion also forced Rush's fellow Pennsylvania Signers to flee. One of these, George Clymer, had been a rich merchant of Philadelphia. Clymer was a firm patriot, but always a reluctant public figure. He had met Washington as early as 1765, and was a leader in protests against taxed tea in 1773. But Clymer, with an outwardly cool and indolent manner, never wanted office, although he was strongly in favor of declaring independence in 1776. In office, Clymer never appeared to care what his constituents thought. With Wilson, he favored representative democracy, and once said: *A representative of the people is appointed to think for and not with his constituents.* With this firm opinion, he signed the Declaration. He also put all of his specie into Continental bills of credit, and assisted Robert Morris to raise money. This act cost him heavily.

He was the official who received, and made provision for, the horde of Hessian prisoners Washington captured at Trenton. These men were put out on farms, and generally well treated; many, in fact, never returned to Europe after the war.

When the British marched through eastern Pennsylvania in 1777, Clymer's home was deliberately ransacked; a party deviated from the line of march to seek the house out and destroy Clymer's goods and provisions as an act of political terrorism. Clymer's wife and children hid in the woods while the furnishings were burned.

Although Clymer never conceded an inch to popular sentiment he failed to share, in later years, during the conservative political reaction in Pennsylvania, he was sent to the United States Congress. Rush's own comment on Clymer, who was his patient and friend, was, *the mould in which this man's mind was cast . . . was seldom used.*

The three remaining Signers' homes lay outside the British axis of advance. George Ross was a lawyer, who settled in Lancaster. He was related by marriage to two other Signers, James Wilson and George Read of Delaware. Ross' political career began in 1768, with his election to the Assembly. As the representative of a western constituency, Ross showed interest in Indian affairs, opposing many of the Quaker–eastern Pennsylvania interests, who showed no concern with either frontier protection or the western advance. He also came into strong conflict with the governor and Proprietary party, although he was, in the west, generally considered to have Tory leanings. In 1774 he was sent to the strongly moderate First Continental Congress. He did not appear publicly as a Whig until 1775, and this led to his return in 1776. Ross was a good speaker, with considerable wit, and drew attention. But he also *disliked business, and hence possessed but little influence in Congress,* as Rush wrote.

Ross is remembered chiefly, though ironically, through his connection with the first American flag. The flag was actually designed by Francis Hopkinson of New Jersey, the Signer of many talents. But a committee of Ross, Robert Morris, and Washington is said to have called on a niece of Ross's by marriage, Betsy Griscom Ross, in early 1777. She agreed to sew the flag, and even suggested some parts of the design. This red, white, and blue emblem, with thirteen stripes and stars, was adopted by Congress on June 14, henceforth to be known as Flag Day.

Ross's health failed in 1777, and he was forced to retire from public life. On his return to Lancaster, he was offered a presentation of silver plate worth £150 for his services. Ross refused it, stating it was the duty of every man *to contribute by every means within his power to the welfare of his country without expecting pecuniary rewards.* He died soon afterward, in 1779.

Jas. Smith

James Smith was born in Ireland sometime between 1713 and 1722; Smith was eccentric and refused to give his age. He emigrated as a child with his father, secured a good education, and studied law. He began practice in the western counties, up against Indian territory. Smith, like most of the new blood sent to Congress in 1776 from Pennsylvania, was a representative of the "radical" west.

He settled in York, developed an ironworks, and made a considerable fortune. Although he is described by Rush as erratic in his politics, Smith was an early Whig. He expected trouble, and was responsible for raising and training the first corps of minutemen in Pennsylvania. He was appointed colonel and later brigadier of militia, but he was too old to serve actively. As a representative of the newer, democratic faction, he was sent to Congress in 1776. His main services there seem to have been more entertaining than political. He spoke in an Irish brogue, and frequently had the House laughing at his funny stories.

When he entered Congress, Smith put his business in the hands of superintendents. These two men proceeded to mismanage the ironworks, and Smith lost the equivalent of £5,000, then an enormous sum. Smith left Congress in 1778, though he served in the state government, and as a judge, in later years.

Geo. Taylor

George Taylor, also Irish, was a truer representative of the western Pennsylvania spirit than Smith. Taylor had the distinction of having worked his way up to wealth and prominence from the status of emigrant bond servant.

Taylor, the son of a Protestant clergyman, had failed a crucial examination in medicine. Discouraged, without a sixpence in his pocket, he wandered down to the waterfront in Dublin and took passage on an English ship for America. To pay his passage, he followed a then-common practice; he bound himself over as a redemptioner or bond servant. On arrival at Philadelphia, the shipmaster sold his contract to a local citizen, for whom Taylor was legally obligated to work without pay until his debt was repaid. Since there were open lands and little poverty in America, labor was short. There was frequently spirited bidding for redemptioners' contracts at the dock.

Taylor was bound over to an ironmaster named Savage at Durham, and put to work feeding coal into a blast furnace. But Savage was a perceptive, kindly man, who noticed the blisters on young Taylor's hands, and also realized his servant possessed some education. Learning of Taylor's background, Savage inquired if he would not prefer a pen to a shovel, and Taylor became a trusted clerk in Savage's business.

A few years later, Savage died, and George Taylor married his widow. He thus came into the ironworks, but more important, he ran the business successfully. He moved to Northampton County and opened a large ironmill. He was able to build a fine house on the Lehigh River, and in 1764 was sent to the legislature. Taylor was a strong Whig, opposed to the eastern interests and the Proprietary, or Governor's Party. He became one of the dominant group of democratically-minded westerners who pushed the colony toward full independence. He was on the Committee of Safety in 1775, and served in Congress between 1776 and March, 1777.

Rush said of Taylor, *A respectable country gentleman, but not much distinguished in any way in Congress.* Taylor's absence in Congress—he went with the main body to Baltimore—caused his business to decline rapidly, and when he died in 1781 he was no longer wealthy and already obscure. Yet George Taylor remained a lasting symbol of social mobility in America, with Roger Sherman of Connecticut and Franklin.

In the aftermath of the battles in Pennsylvania in 1777, Dr. Rush fell into spirited controversy with the Director of Hospitals, his superior as surgeon-general. Rush considered the abominable conditions of Revolutionary military hospitals intolerable; the mortality rate was high even by contemporary standards. He sent protests to the Director and, over this official's head, to Washington. He wrote that he loved his country, and the *brave men who had offered their lives for its defense too well to shrink from what I conceived to be my duty upon this occasion.*

Rush's humanitarianism did spark some reforms, but the Congress refused to sustain his protests against the Director. Feeling he could not work with the man, Rush resigned his commission in early 1778. And now, feeling that General Washington was failing to win the war, Rush entered into the most controversial action of his career. He joined the "Conway Cabal," a conspiracy to replace Washington as commander-in-chief. Rush wrote a letter to Patrick Henry criticizing Washington. Although the letter was not signed, Henry, and Washington, to whom Henry forwarded the letter, recognized the doctor's hand. George Washington accused Rush of disloyalty, and this incident ended Rush's military services to the Revolution.

He did however, continue a long and distinguished public and medical career in Philadelphia: he was professor of medicine at the University of Pennsylvania, a member of the state convention, founder of Dickinson College in Carlisle, president of the local medical society, and a leader in the Abolition and Bible Societies. In his last years he was also Treasurer of the United States Mint.

The Signers suffered from British persecution in direct proportion to the exposure of their property and persons to enemy action. Thus New Englanders such as John Hancock and Samuel Adams had their most dangerous moments before the Declaration. The British evacuated Boston on March 17, 1776, and thereafter New England was not a major theater of war. There were isolated incidents and raids, as when a British squadron seized Newport, Rhode Island, in December, 1776. William Ellery's house was burned to the ground by the enemy on the same night that Washington crossed the Delaware.

Many of the Signers from this area suffered hardships, wounds, and dangers as members of the armed forces; and all of them risked exactly as much as the Signers farther south. If the British won the war, all stood to be ruined, if not publicly hanged.

The fortunes of war largely spared the Delaware and Maryland Signers, who on August 2, 1776, had been considered among the most exposed of all. These provinces had long coastlines, and the British had complete command of the sea. Punitive raids, such as the one on Falmouth, and the bombardment of Norfolk, were already in progress. However, Delaware and Maryland were spared, although one Signer, the reluctant George Read, had a narrow escape.

Read was born gentry, descended from Sir Thomas Read, an affluent Anglo-Irish squire. He inherited his father's estate on the Christiana River in what was then the *three counties on Delaware*, part of Pennsylvania; however, he gave up the double share of this estate he was due under provincial law as eldest son, and took up the practice of law. He was admitted to the bar, and the formidable competition of the Philadelphia lawyers, in 1753, when he was just nineteen.

He faced Benjamin Chew, John Dickinson, George Ross, and Thomas McKean in court, and apparently won enough cases to become successful. He was a man of highly independent mind, whose actions were not always predictable, although he earned the reputation of "honest lawyer." Although one of his maxims was that *men of ambition should never marry*, he did. His bride was the sister of Signer George Ross. In 1763, when the Delaware counties were organized into a separate colony, he became Delaware's first attorney-general. By 1765 he was in the provincial assembly and quite prominent in local affairs.

Read was a Whig, but he considered his opposition directed only to the British Parliament. He was firm in defending American rights. Before the shooting started, he helped raise $900 in Delaware to support the Boston Sons of Liberty. Samuel Adams thanked him in a letter, in which the term *fellow countryman* was used.

He was chosen for the First Congress with Caesar Rodney and Thomas McKean. Thereafter he was in Congress throughout the war, except for his term as president or governor, of Delaware. Read opposed the Declaration, for reasons that have never been made clear. He stubbornly voted against it on the last day, when his two colleagues joined the majority. His patriotism was never questioned; it was thought he followed his conscience to the last. He signed the Declaration, though he was warned by Joseph Galloway, the former American leader who had turned Loyalist, *You are signing with a halter around your neck.* Read answered that he was prepared to meet that consequence, and he almost did.

When President John McKinly of Delaware was captured by the British at Wilmington, Read became acting governor. It is generally admitted that his efforts to support the war in Delaware were paramount at this time. The state was exposed by its long coastlines; the Delaware River was under constant enemy patrol. The British made a determined effort to capture Read—they forced his wife, who now had a large and still infant family to hide in various homes and villages about the state. And on one occasion, while Read was attempting to get his family safely across the Delaware, he was almost taken.

With his wife, children, and mother, Read was stopped on the river by a British barge. Coolly, the Delaware President gave an assumed name, and told the sailors he was a Loyalist country gentleman merely trying to reach his estate on the far shore. The fact that the Read family, bag and baggage, was piled into his boat caused the British to believe him. With good humor, the Royal Navy not only did not detain him, but even assisted him to land. Sailors carried his baggage, and his wife, mother, and children up the bank. Not until months later did the Navy realize it had let one of the most hunted Americans in the Middle Colonies slip through its fingers.

In later years, Read was instrumental in promoting the rights of small states at the Constitutional Convention of 1787, securing equal representation in the United States Senate. He was twice Senator, and died as Chief Justice of Delaware in 1798. His children, grandchildren, and great-grandchildren were prominent in the service of the United States.

Another Delaware delegate, Caesar Rodney, was one of the more tragic figures of the Revolution. The Rodneys traced their ancestry back to a family on the fringes of the English aristocracy, ruined by the seventeenth-century civil wars. The first Rodney in America, William, settled in the County of Kent *on Delaware*. Originally a Swedish colony, Kent was then briefly under the Dutch, and finally incorporated into Pennsylvania. The three counties which later became the State of Delaware were granted a separate assembly in 1702, largely though William Rodney's efforts. Caesar Rodney was born at Dover in 1728, the oldest of eight children. Through the existing laws on primogeniture and entail, he inherited his father's considerable landed estate.

As a member of the gentry, Rodney accepted public service. He was High Sheriff of Kent in 1758, then a magistrate, and in the seventeen-sixties, when Delaware was formed into a separate province, he entered the legislature and became its speaker.

Rodney never married. He had developed a malignancy of the face, and when he began his political career he was forced to wear a green silk scarf over part of his face and one eye. His colleagues remembered him as *an animated skeleton, with a bandaged head.*

Rodney was a strong Whig. With Thomas McKean he arrived early at understanding the need for independence; John Adams, in 1774, said that Rodney, McKean, and Patrick Henry *appeared to see more clearly to the end of the business than any others,* or at least were more *candid and explicit* than any others in the First Congress.

Rodney was at Dover working for independence against strong Tory opposition in Delaware when the crucial vote on Lee's motion was carried by the majority of the whole and then put over till the next day in the hope of greater unanimity. McKean and George Read split, and only an express letter to Rodney from McKean allowed Delaware to join the colonies' solid front. Caesar Rodney rode all night —80 miles—through a thunderstorm to cast his deciding ballot in the Delaware delegation. He met McKean at the door of the State House in Philadelphia—booted, spurred, and mud-splattered.

Thomas McKean, who was born in Chester County, Pennsylvania, was of Scots-Irish stock. He took up the practice of law in New Castle County, Delaware, and became active in the politics of that province, going to the Assembly in 1762. His first wife, who died in 1773, was a daughter of Joseph Borden of New Jersey; thus he was a brother-in-law of Francis Hopkinson. McKean showed a strong belief in American rights and was, as Adams wrote, an early battler for independence. He bore the brunt of this battle in the Delaware Assembly.

After signing, McKean stayed in Congress throughout the war, except for one year. In 1779 he wrote John Adams that he had been *hunted like a fox by the enemy . . . compelled to move my family five times in a few months, and at last fixed them in a little log-house on the banks of the Susquehanna. . . .* Here they were harassed and forced to move again by Indians. McKean was to be claimed both by Delaware and Pennsylvania. In later years he returned to the state of his birth, and was governor of Pennsylvania from 1799 to 1808.

Caesar Rodney, who had no immediate family, was not chased about by the British, but he suffered in an entirely different way. At the beginning of the American-British troubles, Rodney sought medical attention in Philadelphia. He was told that there was no help for him in the Colonies and advised to sail to Europe. There was, of course, no cure for his cancer in either London or Edinburgh, but neither his doctors nor his relatives knew this. They begged him to drop politics and try to save his life. When Rodney signed the Declaration he knew he was cutting himself off from any possible medical relief treatment in the British Isles.

Despite his affliction and pain, Rodney was an active patriot leader. As a brigadier of Delaware militia, he was so efficient and thorough in raising and supplying troops that Washington called the Delaware Line the best in his Continental Army. Rodney was unfit for active service, but after Brandywine he personally led the Delaware Militia north to assist Washington. His support of Delaware troops, and the measures he adopted within the state, were extremely effective in carrying on the war.

Rodney served four years as governor of his state. He never expressed complaint or regret for his choice. When, after terrible pain, he died in 1784, a few months after the final peace, his family and friends considered him a true casualty of the Revolution.

The Marylanders were fortunate. Although there were raids, alarms, and blockades along the Chesapeake, the British never attempted to march across the colony. The Maryland Signers, Samuel Chase, William Paca, Thomas Stone, and Charles Carroll, who risked more wealth and property than any other man in America, were not forced to suffer for their act of courage.

Samuel Chase

Samuel Chase, nicknamed "Bacon Face" because of his red, mottled complexion, was the son of an Episcopal clergyman. His father gave him a fine classical education, and he was admitted to the Maryland Bar in 1761 at the age of twenty. Chase achieved considerable success in practice at Annapolis; he married, and was elected to the Maryland Assembly in 1764.

Chase had a good intellect, but a turbulent disposition. He was a man who not only liked a political fight, but went out of his way to seek one. In the Assembly, where he was to serve twenty years, Chase was noted for his independent ideas and an *uncourtly bearing towards the royal governor and the court party.*

Chase's first great argument with the authorities came with the Stamp Act. He joined the Sons of Liberty who sprang up everywhere. At Annapolis, the members of this group forcibly broke into the public offices in which the excise stamps were stored, burned them, and also hung the stamp officer in effigy. Chase took a prominent part in this action and made no attempt to conceal it.

The mayor of Annapolis branded the young Mr. Chase as a *busy, restless incendiary, ringleader of mobs, a foul-mouthed and inflaming son of discord.*

Chase had his reply publicly printed, stating that the Sons of Liberty might have been a mob, but that they contained *men of reputation and merit* in far greater degree than the *tools of power, emerged from obscurity and basking in proprietary sunshine*—the mayor and his kind.

Wm Paca

Shortly afterward, Chase was joined in the legislature by his lifelong friend and political associate, William Paca. Paca was a year older, but he was described by Benjamin Rush (who had no great respect for Chase's mind, either) as:

. . . *A good tempered worthy Man, with a sound Understanding which he was too indolent to exercise. He therefore gave himself up to be directed both in his political Opinions and conduct by Saml Chase who had been the friend of his youth, & for whom he retained a regard in every Stage of his life.*

This description is not entirely fair to Paca, although he did follow Chase's opinions. Paca was very much a patriot, and personally exerted much influence in Maryland in the struggle against the proprietary, or British party. Paca's family, which possibly was of Italian origin, held extensive lands and was well-to-do by the beginning of the eighteenth century. Paca took a degree at the College of Philadelphia in 1759, had further training at law in London, at the Inner Temple, and married Mary Chew, a very wealthy Philadelphia girl, in 1763. A year later he was admitted to the provincial bar in Annapolis.

Paca and Chase became fast friends in Annapolis and in the legislature after 1768. Both were elegant, well-dressed, and well-spoken young men; their persons and manner, as Rush said, were very acceptable. Rush and some of the New Englanders felt that they owed much of their success in *political life* to this alone. However, they were early rebels against proprietary privilege in the Colony of Maryland and influenced all ranks of men.

There was a gentlemanly gaiety associated with the Maryland opposition that was lacking in other areas, which perhaps led to the outside feeling that the elegant Marylanders were frivolous. On one occasion Paca and Chase organized a public protest against a governor's edict. Paca copied the official proclamation on a scrap of paper; then, with a large body of Annapolis citizenry he and Chase led the way to a mock gallows erected on the edge of town. The edict was *executed* by being strung up; hats were ceremoniously doffed as it *expired*. Then, *after a decent interval*, Paca had the remains cut down, placed in a mock coffin, and buried under the gallows while a small cannon, on a Paca-owned schooner in the Bay, fired a salute. Afterwards, Paca's liberal purse opened the taverns, and a wild celebration was held, to the governor's fury.

Chase, Paca, and another Marylander, Charles Carroll, gained fame, in 1770, when the Maryland Assembly passed a bill lowering the salaries of Crown officials and the Anglican clergy, who at this period were supported by the state. Chase voted for the bill although it reduced his father's income. However, the act was opposed in the Governor's Council, which acted as the upper house; many Council members were adversely affected. Governor Robert Eden ended the political impasse by dissolving the Assembly and continuing the former stipends by edict. This was within the governor's powers, but it aroused much popular feeling against the Proprietary government.

Chase, Paca, and Thomas Johnson became known throughout the colony over an exchange of letters with one Daniel Dulany and another citizen, James Holliday, over the not-quite-expired issue. However, the letter-writing contest was won by another gentleman, who earned even greater notice. Daniel Dulaney, for the Proprietors, had written a purported series of exchanges between "First Citizen," a sort of straw man, and "Second Citizen," the name he chose for himself. In Dulany's writings, "First Citizen," who took the popular side, naturally came off worse. Now, Charles Carroll of Carrollton, as he called himself to distinguish himself from his father and cousins of the same name, published a series of articles signed "First Citizen," in which the demolished straw man rallied strongly.

Carroll was a true grandee. He was born at Annapolis, descendant of an important family who had emigrated from Ireland at about the time of the Revolution of 1688. The Carrolls were Roman Catholics and had held offices under James II. However, they did not come as destitute refugees; the first Charles Carroll arrived holding the Proprietor's commission as attorney-general for the colony. At a time when Catholics were persecuted in England and Ireland, Carroll had decided to emigrate to Maryland in search of religious freedom. This province had been originally founded by the Baltimores as a refuge for English Catholics; the second Lord Baltimore, in 1649, had issued a famous Toleration Act for the Colony, which stated: *Noe person or psons whatsoever within this Province . . . professing to believe in Jesus Christ, shall from henceforth*

*bee any waies troubled, Molested or discountenanced for
in respect to his or her religion.*

However, while the Calverts, or Baltimore family, retained Proprietary rights and privileges like the Penn family
in Pennsylvania, Maryland rapidly turned into a predominantly Protestant, rather than Catholic, colony. Emigra-
tion into seventeenth- and eighteenth-century America was
overwhelmingly Protestant, or became Protestant; by 1776
there were no more than 30,000 Catholics in all the colonies combined. Unhappily and ironically, in the eighteenth century the early refugees again lost many of their
civil rights. Restrictive legislation, similar to that of the
other British colonies was enacted: Roman priests were
barred from holding public services; laymen were disenfranchised; Catholic schools were abolished, and Catholic
landholders were subject to double taxation. One act, which
authorized children to be taken from the homes of Catholic parents, does not seem ever to have been enforced,
however; and in the years preceding the Revolution, the
other laws and restrictions were still on the books, but,
like the strict property requirement for voting, not generally enforced. This lax prosecution, in the growing spirit
of Enlightenment, stayed many Catholics from leaving
America, which at one time Charles Carroll's father con-
templated.

In 1718 it was recorded that Carroll's grandfather, because of his public services, was one of a small group of
Catholics specifically exempted from disqualification in
public affairs due to religion. Carroll himself, however,
was barred from becoming a lawyer or holding political
office when he came of age. Despite this, religion, by the
seventeen-seventies, was no longer an important political

factor in Maryland. In the prevailing Enlightenment—and the Deism of many leaders—there seems to have been little or no religious antagonism between some very disparate groups. Anglicans and Congregationalists, or Presbyterians and Baptists. Charles Carroll was a friend of Samuel Chase, the son of a clergyman, and closely associated with Thomas Stone, the fourth Maryland Signer, who ironically enough was a descendent of William Stone, Oliver Cromwell's governor of Maryland.

Carroll, the scion of an almost kingly, if minority, family, was raised in great red-brick mansion houses and country seats in the beautiful Maryland countryside. He was taught by his mother until he was ten, then sent to one of the clandestine schools run by the Jesuits on Augustine Herman's plantation. One of his classmates in this school was his cousin "Jacky" John Carroll, who was later to become the first Roman Catholic bishop in America.

In 1751, unable to get the kind of education his family desired in America's basically denominational and Protestant colleges, Carroll was sent off to France. He studied at the College de St. Omer in French Flanders, where his father had gone. Afterward, he attended Louis-le-grand Collège in Paris, studied Roman law at Bourges, and spent five years in London, reading English common law at Temple Bar. In 1765 he finally returned home. He was small, slender, with handsome features and graceful movements; the dancing and fencing masters of France had taught him well.

His father deeded him Carrollton Manor, a ten-thousand-acre tract of land in Frederick County. The development of this tract made Carroll the richest man in Maryland, and probably in America. At the same time, he was caught up in the furor over the Stamp Act. Carroll, despite his years abroad, took an immediate American stance and soon was discussing *our oppressive Laws.*

He wrote friends in England that force would not make Americans *depart from the essential right of internal taxation without which our property would be at ye mercy of every rapacious minister,* and that *in these times of necessity and oppression it is a duty every man of fortune owes his country to set an example of frugality and industry.*

Young Carroll took a keen interest in developing politics, but for some years all he could do was write letters explaining the American view to people in England. His religion barred him from holding office or standing for the Assembly. If a majority of the gentlemen of Maryland had no fear of him, it would be a mistake to consider that tolerance ran deeply throughout the entire population. It was to be some years before the independent colonies removed all religious tests, or disestablished churches. Carroll married a cousin, Molly Darnall, whose family was also long in Maryland, and contented himself with an active social life in Annapolis. He became a member of the Homony Club, whose members included Paca, Chase, and even Robert Eden, who had married into the Baltimore family and become the royal governor.

The Dulany dialogue opened up an avenue of action which Carroll seized upon avidly. Daniel Dulany was well known as a member of Robert Eden's Council and as secretary of the colony. Carroll, in the Maryland *Gazette* in early 1773, under the name "First Citizen," wrote that the words Dulany had originally put in "his" mouth were incorrectly reported. The new version ably supported the Assembly, rather than the governor, in the salary-stipend quarrel.

This brought on a literary battle between Carroll and Dulany, as "First Citizen" and "Antilon." The animosity ran deep; it was personal and familial as well as political. Carroll went beyond the present controversy, striking to the heart of the matter: *In a land of freedom . . . arbitrary execution of prerogative will not, must not, be endured.* This was a direct attack on the Royal prerogative, as exercised by the governor, who by this time was no longer a fellow club member, or a friend.

Dulany, outclassed, made a serious error. As "Antilon" he attacked Carroll personally, questioning his *citizenship* and his religion. This boomeranged. The identity of "First Citizen" became public knowledge, and it surprised many Marylanders who would have supposed Carroll's fortune and Jesuitical education might have given him hierarchical views. The language of "First Citizen," attacking all prerogative that was not democratically approved, startled even many of his associates who had known his identity all along. Carroll won the debate overwhelmingly in the popular mind. The letters made him First Citizen of Maryland in fact, and in local elections, in 1773, were the cause of a landslide success for the Patriot party. William Paca and Matthias Hammond thanked Carroll in writing for his part, and the Assembly marched to Carroll's Annapolis house in July, 1773, as a gesture of gratitude.

In May, 1774, with the Boston Port Bill, Carroll was appointed to the Maryland Committee of Correspondence, his first public post.

He declined an appointment to the First Congress, but worked actively behind the scenes to push Maryland toward independence. Carroll was startlingly clear-minded; along with Benjamin Franklin he was a preëminent example of an American man of the world. When Samuel

Chase said, with satisfaction, that the patriot party had completely written the gubernatorial party down, Carroll wearily asked, *Do you think that writing will settle the question between us?*

Chase, startled, said, to be sure. They had won every debate in the Assembly, and in the press—although the governor still ruled by edict. *What else can we resort to?*

The bayonet, Carroll said bluntly. He stated his belief that the arguments of the American leadership, including his own, *would only raise the feelings of the people to that pitch when open war would be eagerly espoused.* These words, spoken several years before Lexington and Concord, were entirely true, and ominously prophetic. Whether they understood it or not, the American gentry was fomenting revolution, and it was a revolution that eventually would go beyond mere separation from the Crown. A cause that was taken up in the name of freedom would have to see freedom extended, not only for the gentry, but further down the social scale, too.

Again, when an Englishman wrote him angrily and arrogantly that *six thousand English soldiers will march from one end of your continent to the other.* Carroll replied: *So they may—but they will be masters of the spot only on which they camp.* No better description of the Revolution, which was really a great guerrilla campaign, in which the professional British forces found themselves opposed by a majority of the people, was ever formulated, then or afterward. Washington kept active rebellion alive by keeping a small force in the field, but he was rarely able to give effective battle. The British marched almost where they willed—but never found the thousands of Tories they had hoped for—they held only the enclaves on which British bayonets stood.

Carroll's wealth, prestige, and example worked a powerful effect in Maryland, where the idea of independence was slow of acceptance. As late as May, 1776, the Assembly instructed its delegates to the Second Congress to oppose separation. One great factor in Maryland was the popularity of the governor, Robert Eden, who despite his earlier arbitrary acts, ruled firmly and spoke softly in the crisis. Carroll's and Chase's great contribution to the Revolution, was not in voting for independence in July, 1776, they were in Maryland, getting these instructions changed. Carroll's own influence was considered decisive in this victory.

Although he had been elected overwhelmingly to the Second Congress in January, 1775, and had taken part in the ill-fated American expedition to separate Canada from Britain that year, his major service was in his own state.

The Marylanders, due to the flow of the war, lived in comparative peace. Carroll did visit Valley Forge in support of Washington, and he was one of the men whose influence and activities broke the "Conway Cabal" to replace the commander-in-chief. William Paca spent thousands of dollars of his own money supplying troops. In honor of this, the Society of the Cincinnati voted him a vice-presidency of the organization, although he never held a commission in the army. He became governor of Maryland in 1782. Samuel Chase fell into disfavor in 1778, through a speculative attempt to corner flour, but afterward died as a justice of the United States Supreme Court.

Charles Carroll enjoyed a long life of public service, finally retiring from the Senate at sixty-three. One of his granddaughters married the Marquis of Wellesley, the brother of the Duke of Wellington. Wellesley became lord lieutenant, or viceroy of Ireland, and thus a descendent of Irish refugees in America reigned over the old country during the Ascendancy, a fact which Carroll regarded with dry good humor. When he died, in 1832 at the age of ninety-one, four years after having formally opened the first section of the Baltimore & Ohio Railroad, he had two distinctions. He was still the richest man in America, and he was the last of the Signers to die.

Thos. Stone

Thomas Stone, the fourth Maryland Signer, was always closely associated with the other three, but he was never as flamboyant, nor did he enjoy as much prominence. Stone was born at Pointon Manor in 1743 and was educated for law. Like the other Signers, he was a strong Whig. He served in the Congress, and later, as a member of the Constitutional Convention. His career was cut short by death at the age of 43.

End Worth Mo

Two years of active warfare and maneuver in the Middle Colonies, in this great campaign of a people against foreign rule, still resulted in a form of stalemate. The British had New York; they were to hold it until after the peace treaty was signed. But Howe's capture of Philadelphia in September, 1777, proved ephemeral. The British were unable to destroy Washington's Continentals, who suffered through Valley Forge a few miles away. Howe controlled only the region his troops patrolled; he held Philadelphia, but no other part of Pennsylvania.

Meanwhile, the grandiose scheme to separate New England from the other colonies had ended in British defeat at Saratoga. The capture of General John Burgoyne and his entire army was probably the single most decisive American victory of the war. Saratoga convinced the French Court that America could not lose, and Benjamin Franklin's adroit diplomacy soon had the French almost begging to sign an alliance. When the French treaty of alliance was signed, the whole complexion of the American Revolution changed. The British were now not only engaged with rebellious colonials, but with a great European power. The French war, which became almost world-wide, occupied the British and diverted troops and ships elsewhere. French money, munitions, and sea power, at a critical time, made Yorktown possible, and French soldiers were present in the final campaign. The great guerrilla war staged by Washington was facing collapse by 1780, because the American economy was collapsing. Without the French alliance, at best, the stalemate would have continued; at worst, the Americans would have had to make some accommodation with the Crown.

General Sir William Howe realized his 1777 campaign was a failure; he had not ended the rebellion. Howe had never had much enthusiasm for the war; now he virtually seceded from it. He was replaced in command by General Sir Henry Clinton in 1778.

Clinton was by nature gloomy and cautious. The orders he now received from Whitehall must have *traumatized him*, as one historian wrote. Clinton was ordered to abandon Philadelphia, but to hold New York and Newport, while detaching several thousand of his finest regulars for duty in the West Indies and Florida, against the French and their Spanish allies. This meant virtual abandonment of British effort in the New England and Middle Atlantic states. The continuing blockade and naval actions along the coast could not be decisive without a sustained land effort.

Marching in retreat across New Jersey to New York, Clinton barely avoided a severe setback at Monmouth, in June, 1778. Back in New York, he found Washington on his heels. The Continentals could not attack New York and defeat the British regulars, but they could, and did, deny them the countryside. After three years of effort, the British were back where they had begun in the summer of 1775. They held enclaves and commanded the coast.

Their greatest assets in this stalemate were not their armies, but the blockade and the weakness of the American confederation government. The states were not truly united; the Continental government had no power to command or tax. Credit, finance, and the money economy fell apart. Although the Northern states were unconquered, they were neutralized, and Washington, in 1779, warned that he might have to break off operations for a year, for lack of economic support.

The new British strategy was to accept the stand-off in the North and reopen the war in the South, where the numerous harbors, the milder climate, and the hope that there were more Tories all encouraged George Sackville, Lord Germain, Secretary of State for the American Colonies. Germain felt the softer American South could be rolled up. It was not an impossible, or even bad, strategy, but it did have two disadvantages. Holding enclaves in the North while campaigning in the South meant a division of British forces, which were never quite large enough for the entire job. Also, such a strategy demanded excellent communications between the areas of operations and full control of the seas. It apparently did not enter Germain's mind that either could be lost.

Because it seemed weaker and more exposed, the Royal Colony of Georgia was selected to receive the first British blow.

The movement of Georgia into rebellion followed the history of the other colonies, although Georgia was among the last to become restive. It was the last province to be settled and organized under the British flag. Georgia was first established as a colony under General James Oglethorpe in 1733, and only became a royal province in 1752, upon surrender of the original charter. At the time of the Revolution, Georgia consisted of only eight parishes or counties, extending about one hundred miles along the Atlantic, and approximately twice that distance up the Savannah River. It had contacts with the older and richer Colony of South Carolina, but to most Georgians Massachusetts Bay seemed more remote than London. Georgia had thus not yet gone through the Americanization process common to most other colonies in the seventeenth century. The path to revolution was blazed by a small but highly influential group of men struggling against caution, conservatism, and inertia.

Lyman Hall

One factor that hastened the Americanization of Georgia was the resettlement of many Virginians, New Englanders, and others along this frontier. These families brought their biases and ideals with them to the far south. One such transplanted New Englander was Lyman Hall.

Hall was a Connecticut Yankee and a graduate of Yale College. After an early stab at the ministry, Hall took up medicine. In the seventeen-fifties, when he was about thirty years of age, Hall and his second wife moved to South Carolina. A few years afterward, Hall joined a group of some forty resettled New England families at Sunbury, in St. John's Parish, Georgia. Here he was the only doctor; he acquired a large medical practice, a plantation, and Negro slaves.

St. John's was a New England enclave, and Hall himself had deep New England connections. John Hancock and Dorothy Quincy had been married at his first wife's brother's house at Fairfield, Connecticut. Therefore, the promulgation of the Intolerable Acts, aimed primarily at Boston and Massachusetts, aroused Hall and his neighbors more strongly than it did many other Georgians. Through 1774, the British ministry had taken no measures specifically prejudicial to the southernmost colony. The royal governor, Sir James Wright, was both intelligent and humane, and his Executive Council contained men of firmness, talent, and good sense as well as partisan appointees. Governor and upper house thus held Georgia firmly in control in 1774, when the reaction to the Intolerable Acts spread through America.

There was a reaction in the Georgia Assembly, which formed a Committee of Correspondence to communicate with Massachusetts and Virginia. A public meeting to discuss the worsening American situation was called in July, by the following notice in a Savannah newspaper:

The critical situation to which British colonies in America are likely to be reduced, from the alarming and arbitrary imposition of the late acts of the British Parliament, respecting the town of Boston, as well as the acts at present, that extend to the raising of a perpetual revenue, without the consent of the people or their representatives, is considered as an object extremely important at this critical juncture, and particularly calculated to deprive the American subjects of their constitutional rights and liberties as a part of the British Empire. It is therefore requested that all persons within the limits of this province do attend, at the Liberty Pole at Tondee's Tavern in Savannah on Wednesday . . . in order that said matters may be taken under consideration, and such other constitutional measures pursued, as may then appear to be most eligible.

> NOBLE W. JONES
> ARCHIBALD BULLOCH
> JOHN HOUSTOUN
> GEORGE WALTON

This meeting was held; there were lively debates. Dr. Hall attended as a representative of St. John's Parish, and he concurred that correspondence he started among the parishes of Georgia in an attempt to have Georgia join the other colonies in protest.

The royal governor, however, realized that Georgia as a whole was not enthusiastic about supporting Boston, and he adopted a clever political stratagem. He sent messages to each parish, berating no one, but simply requesting a pledge of allegiance to His Majesty, King George III. Since the American rationale at this period stressed loyalty to the Crown, though not Parliament, this pledge was impossible to ignore. The parishes responded honestly, and this simple act did a great deal to sober Georgians and damp the revolutionary ire. The Georgia Assembly sent no representatives to the First Continental Congress of 1774.

Further, in the Provincial Convention at Savannah in January, 1775, Georgia refused to adopt the Continental Association authorized by the First Congress at Philadelphia. This Association pledged a voluntary embargo on trade with Great Britain until the dispute should be resolved. Dr. Hall sat in this convention, and here he broke with every other parish, by supporting the measure strongly.

Hall rode back to his parish and spread his dissatisfaction in a mass meeting with his constituents. St. John's resolved to apply to the South Carolina Committee of Correspondence for permission to join with that colony in observing the Nonimportation Act. However, though South Carolina had kind words for the Georgians' patriotism and urged them to keep up their *laudable exertions*, the older colony denied Hall's request. The terms of the Continental Association forbade South Carolina to join with a fragment of another province; the articles spelled out that each colony must be represented on an undivided basis.

Frustrated here, Dr. Hall and his parish passed a local resolution binding the residents of St. John's to stop trading through Savannah, or with the rest of Georgia, except for utter necessities. St. John's withdrew from the provincial Assembly, and thus virtually seceded from the Royal Colony of Georgia on its own. The next move was to send Lyman

Hall to Philadelphia, as St. John's delegate to the Second Continental Congress. The governor described this act in a letter to the Earl of Dartmouth, prophesying that the *poor, insignificant fanatics* at St. John's would be brushed off again.

Hall arrived at Philadelphia May 13, 1775. Here he created some confusion; there was no precedent for a single county's being represented in this association of colonies or provinces. It was obvious that Hall could not speak for all Georgia—but he assumed a certain importance as the sole representative from that colony. Solidarity, or the show of it, was vital. The Congress voted to seat Hall, but with the provision that he might not vote on any roll call by colonies. Georgia was officially listed as absent.

At Philadelphia, Hall stated he had an earnest hope that his colony might soon join with St. John's in supporting the Congress, and in this he was not long disappointed. The coolly competent governor and his reasonable council were being rapidly undermined by British policy. The contemptuous rejection of the First Congress' petitions produced a sour effect in Georgia, as everywhere. The bloodshed around Boston in the spring of 1775 caused great excitement, and also sympathy for the New Englanders. Most disastrous of all, to the governor's hope of keeping Georgia safely for the Crown, was the British Government's decision to harass the colonies by fomenting Indian troubles.

Almost all of Georgia still bordered on Indian country, in restless proximity to the powerful Creek tribe. It is certain that the British ministers who approved arming the Indians never understood the immense repugnance such a policy produced among all American whites, and especially those closest to the Indian frontier. The British policy-makers seemed to know very little of the savagery of American-Indian wars, which had already been in progress for more than a hundred years. But all the American settlers were conscious of massacred families, tomahawked children, and men and women burnt alive; little mercy, in this conflict, was shown by either side. The deliberate fomenting of new uprisings, of setting redmen on white by Crown agents, which began in 1775, caused fewer and fewer Americans to believe the British government was reasonable or right. More and more Georgia settlers became enraged at the Crown, and determined to make common cause of armed resistance with the other colonies.

The Georgia Assembly met several times in the first part of 1775, debating the momentous question. The governor scrupulously kept his hands off the legislature, and this moderation allowed the Loyalist Party to delay final action for some time. Finally, on July 15, 1775, the Georgia Assembly voted to join the Second Congress and elected four more delegates to join Hall, who was now officially confirmed.

Wright urged caution. But he had no power to make concessions or alleviate British policy, and he found himself backed into the same corner as the other royal executives. He had to support the Crown's unpopular acts. As a last resort, he threatened the Assembly with arrest in the name of the King. But he had no troops at his command except a ceremonial detachment and six small warships in Savannah harbor. The angry, now openly rebellious Assembly countered by placing the governor himself under arrest. Wright was paroled on his word of honor; he rationalized that a parole given traitors was not valid and escaped to a King's ship. Thus, at last, Georgia followed the pattern of every other American colony and established the universality of the American experience.

Chasing out the governor did not mean Georgia was ready for independence. The first contingent to the Congress was instructed only to join in a struggle for a *permanent recognition by Great Britain of American rights and claims.*

The first delegation to Philadelphia, besides Dr. Hall, included Archibald Bulloch, John Houstoun, Noble W. Jones, and the Reverend Doctor John Joachim Zubly, a Swiss-born Calvinist minister. Two of these men—one was Bulloch—arrived clad in homespun garments, which a Congressman described as *an Adornment few other Members can boast of.* Of this group, Hall, Houstoun, and Bulloch were in favor of strong action, if John Dickinson's Olive Branch Petition to the King were rejected.

Zubly, however, was apparently affronted by the open talk of full independence and the belligerence he found at Philadelphia among the "violent" party. He wrote a letter secretly to the Governor of Georgia, betraying some secrets of Congress, and urging action to prevent an imminent break between the colonies and the Crown. A copy of this letter came to Samuel Chase's hands; Zubly was accused of treason to the American cause on the floor of Congress. He did not brand the letter as a forgery, but rode out of Philadelphia at once, turned full Tory, and sought asylum on a British man-of-war.

John Houstoun was ordered to ride after him, to arrest Zubly and bring him back for trial. Meanwhile, the letter did no harm, because by this time the Governor of Georgia was himself isolated on a gunboat off the coast.

In February, 1776, the Georgia Provincial Congress re-elected Dr. Hall to Congress and sent two new members north, George Walton and Button Gwinnett. Walton did not reach Philadelphia until late in June. John Houstoun was absent, presumably still on the trail of Zubly. Archibald Bulloch was chosen President of the Georgia Provincial Council, or governor; in April, 1776, he sent the Council's instructions on to Philadelphia. In these new orders there was an important change: due to the *remote Situation* and the delegates *Patriotism, Abilities, Firmness and Integrity,* they were given a free hand to do whatever they thought best for the *common good.* Lyman Hall and Button Gwinnett immediately joined the "violents" under Adams; a letter of Edward Rutledge stated that the whole argument for independence—which he then opposed—was sustained by the *Power of all N. England, Virginia & Georgia.* . . .

Button Gwinnett

Gwinnett was an Englishman, the son of a clergyman in Herefordshire. He emigrated to Savannah; he was established in that town as a merchant by 1765, when he was about thirty years of age. After surveying the prospects of the colony, he decided to become a planter. Gwinnett turned his stock of merchandise into money and purchased St. Catharine's Island, an area of 36 square miles opposite Sunbury, in St. John's Parish. Although he set up as a large planter, Gwinnett remained in considerable debt for this baronial estate.

Gwinnett was a Whig by birth, and never sanguine about the royal prerogative even in England. But he was not sanguine about Americans' chances of successfully opposing the power of Great Britain. He did not join in any of the early resistance movements because he thought they were futile.

All old records indicate that he was swayed into action by the enthusiasm and idealism of Lyman Hall. He was certainly conspicuous in the activist ranks by the summer of 1775, though he did mention to his friends that he believed this stand would result in his and his family's ruin, for his property on St. Catharine's Island was indefensible. With the same gloomy prediction, he accepted election to Congress in 1776. But in company with Hall he was, as even the energetic Doctor wrote, a *Whig to excess.* He hammered for independence, and signed the Declaration.

Geo Walton.

George Walton, who arrived only in time to vote with the majority in July, had a far different background from the other two Georgia delegates. Like them, he was a transplanted British subject, from Virginia. But while Gwinnett and Hall had been born into at least the fringes of the "upper orders" and had received superior educations, Walton's family was desperately poor. He was born in Prince Edward County (some accounts say Frederick), Virginia, around 1741. He was orphaned early, and apprenticed to a carpenter while still a child.

Accounts differ as to how Walton secured his education.

In one, his master was a hard man, who sarcastically refused Walton's request to learn to read, and denied him tapers to study by at night, when his regular work was finished. In this early account young Walton gathered chips and shavings and burned these in place of candles while poring over borrowed books. Another, probably truer, account has it that Walton's carpenter released his apprentice, who was virtually a bond servant, to attend a local school. Either way, Walton's early life was hard; he worked from dawn to dark learning his trade; and like Abraham Lincoln, his education was largely self-acquired. But when his apprenticeship came to an end, Walton had a smattering of learning, callouses on his hands, and a burning desire to rise in life. He left old Virginia, seeking new opportunity in newer Georgia.

He fell in with Henry Young, who was a prominent Georgia lawyer. Young was impressed by Walton's ambition, and agreed that the law was the best means by which a man could improve his station in America. Young took Walton into his office to read law. This proved a long and extremely laborious task. Walton had much to learn or unlearn; he did not know how to speak effectively; he lacked all polish. He persevered, knowing that a colonial American had more opportunity at the bar than anywhere else. Here ability counted, and it was quickly realized—or the lack of it found out. Law was the most respected profession in America; for this reason so many talented young men were called to it, and, because of the intimate connection between law and politics in English-speaking nations, pulled into public life.

George Walton was not admitted to the Georgia bar in Savannah until 1774, when he was at least thirty-three.

In colonial America, where men and careers matured early, he was a dozen years behind his colleagues. He soon caught up, though not at the bar. Walton had acquired a vehement interest in American rights through his study of law; his immediate decision to speak out on the American side cost him the friendship of his mentor Henry Young, who remained Loyalist.

Walton was one of the first Georgia rebels, signing the advertisement for the gathering at Tondee's Tavern in the summer of 1774. He was involved in the Assembly through the next year. When Georgia finally joined the other twelve colonies he was a natural choice for Philadelphia; he was not elected in the first delegation because he was active in the colony, but he was appointed to Congress the next year.

The news of the Declaration did not reach Savannah until August 8, 1776. The actions of their delegates, and the Congress, were received by Georgians with enthusiasm. President Archibald Bulloch read the proclamation first to the Council, and then to the public assembled outside the legislative buildings. It was proclaimed at the Liberty Pole at Tondee's, to the accompaniment of artillery salutes. Among the speeches made to the people was the following: *. . . Let us remember America is free and independent, that she is, and will be, with the blessing of the Almighty, GREAT among the nations of the earth. . . .* Nowhere was the news more joyfully received than in Lyman Hall's and Button Gwinnett's community of St. John's.

Although reëlected to Congress with Hall, Gwinnett and Walton were soon back in Georgia. Walton became a colonel of militia. Button Gwinnett began a short and highly controversial political career.

Many of the Signers, and especially those more prominent in public affairs at home, alternated between Philadelphia and the capitals of their home states. During 1775–1776 every former colony was involved in reorganizing its government and promulgating new constitutions. The acts of liberalization and changes in government which are thought of in connection with the Revolution did not occur on the national level first, but within each state. These local events actually overshadowed Philadelphia in importance; in the end, the reforms, decisions, and positions adopted by the several states formed the pattern of the coming Union. The independent American democracy was first institutionalized on the state level. It was a combination of these institutions and constitutions, from bicameral legislatures to the franchise to the abolition of religious tests, that was later written into the Federal Constitution. Since even the war was hardly more important in many Signers' minds, they were actively caught up in this work.

Button Gwinnett was among those who helped write state constitutions; he was a member of the Georgia Constitutional Convention which adopted a draft in February, 1777. Bulloch died at about this time, and Gwinnett was chosen by the legislature to replace him. As President of Georgia, Button Gwinnett had achieved the pinnacle of political success, after only one full year in public life.

Gwinnett was tall, commanding, and capable, but somewhat imperious of manner and with a short-fused temper. He lacked the charming manner of Lyman Hall and George Walton's bluff honesty. Gwinnett was courageous, but also impatient of opposition to a fault. These traits made him a good rebel, but these, plus the facts of his English birth and meteoric rise to eminence, also made him enemies.

Faced with jealousies among some of Georgia's top men, Button Gwinnett had no tact to soften them; he made them worse.

He also seems to have had a thirst for military glory. Despite holding the Governorship, Gwinnett desired to command the Georgia Line, the Continental brigade being raised for Washington's army. A combination of his opponents in the legislature instead granted the commission to Colonel Lachlan McIntosh. Unfortunately, Gwinnett took this as a personal repudiation and insult. Denied his generalcy, he took out a certain amount of spite on the Georgia military forces, state and Continental alike.

As President, or governor, he refused to permit any military commander the right to courts-martial while on Georgia soil—thus soldiers had to be tried, even for purely military offenses, in civil courts. Discipline suffered, and George Washington himself wrote Gwinnett in protest. Going further, Gwinnett had military officers of high rank hauled before the various state legislative bodies or councils, charged with various alleged offenses. He interfered, or tried to interfere in every military and defense decision, to the point of selecting junior officers for certain missions over the protest of the senior commander concerned. These powers were available to a powerful state governor in that epoch, and, in all fairness, Gwinnett was by no means the only executive who tried to use them. Both Patrick Henry and Thomas Jefferson, neither of whom was a military man, as governors of Virginia regularly interfered with the running of the war.

Gwinnett's obstruction in Georgia helped wreak havoc, however. When Colonel Lachlan McIntosh mounted an attack on British Florida, Gwinnett, exceeding his authority, placed one of McIntosh's own lieutenant-colonels in command of the expedition. Not surprisingly, this expedition met defeat and disaster; the top command positions were filled with dissension. In the aftermath of defeat, Gwinnett was defeated for reelection, after having held the governor's chair only a few months.

The Assembly investigated the McIntosh disaster, and although Gwinnett was sustained, the personal acrimony between the two men led to a duel. Dueling was socially acceptable in every part of America except New England, and in most regions it was virtually mandatory after the passage of insults. Versions differ as to whether Gwinnett challenged McIntosh or vice versa; at any rate, the two met over pistols at twelve paces.

In the discharge both men went down. McIntosh was badly wounded but survived; Button Gwinnett did not. He expired on May 19, 1777, the second Signer to die.

Gwinnett's prophecy of personal ruin, and the ruin of his family, came true. The British seized St. Catharine's Island and his estate, and his wife and daughter apparently did not survive the war. Least known of all the Signers, Button Gwinnett later gained the distinction of leaving the rarest autograph of all.

The first British blow at the American South, under the new policy of 1778, came in December. Lieutenant Colonel Archibald Campbell landed near Savannah with 3,500 men. He took a position between the capital city and the mouth of the Savannah River; he did not intend to attack until reinforcements arrived from Florida under Brigadier Augustin Prevost.

Campbell was himself attacked in this position by about

850 Americans under General Robert Howe. This assault was pressed with great courage, but perhaps not too much good sense. Campbell retaliated by breaking the American onrush with a bayonet charge; then he rolled up the disorganized Americans with a flanking attack. Over half of Howe's troops were killed, wounded, or taken prisoner. This victory permitted Campbell to seize Savannah, then a town of about three thousand, and send more troops upriver to capture Augusta.

George Walton, as a militia officer, fought under Howe. Walton's own unit stood its ground until Walton fell with a musket ball in the thigh; when he fell from his horse his men dissolved. Walton was taken prisoner.

Colonel Campbell treated this distinguished captive with courtesy. He allowed Walton to give his parole, so that he could recover from his serious wound under private care. When Walton had recovered sufficiently, Campbell then incarcerated him at Sunbury.

Meanwhile, the British army overran the Georgia coast an pushed far up the Savannah. Lyman Hall's rice plantation was seized and burned, and all his other property was confiscated in the name of the Crown. The Doctor, who had rushed back from the North, was able to get his family to safety across the Carolina line, but from now through 1782 he was deprived of all income from his estate, and also barred from his practice at St. John's. His family suffered great privations.

The British were willing to exchange George Walton, but because he was a Signer and still a member of Congress they demanded a brigadier general in return. Perhaps not too flatteringly, Congress insisted that Walton was only a colonel of militia and held out for an even exchange, rank for rank. He was eventually exchanged in September, 1779, after his Congressional term expired, for a captain of the Royal Navy.

Released, Walton was appointed governor of Georgia in October, 1779. But this was now an empty honor, because virtually all of the state had been overrun by the enemy. The patriot government was dissolved. The British even installed an effective Royalist regime and seemed to have regained complete control. The best that General Benjamin Lincoln, sent down by Washington to command the Southern Department, could do was guard the South Carolina border. Under this enemy occupation, however, the seemingly pacified province smouldered, and the backcountry flamed into a terrible guerrilla war, which in time extended into the Carolinas.

There was much Tory strength in the South, as the British had thought. It was nowhere dominant, but with the appearance of redcoats it came out in force. Some Scots settlers held for the Crown, just as in upstate New York many small farmers remained Loyalist. These partisan line-ups were based more on local politics than broad ideology or feelings of patriotism. Many Southern backwoodsmen or westerners had no love for the King, but they considered themselves oppressed by tidewater colonial assemblies, by which they were underrepresented and frequently overtaxed. Ironically, but humanly, in parts of the South there occurred a revolution within a revolution; when the eastern-dominated legislatures threw the royal government out, the westerners rebelled and sided with the Crown. The divisions, however, were never clearcut; they cut across class, regional, and, frequently, even family lines. This mixture turned the Southern campaign into a genuine civil war, such as never quite occurred further north, and this factor made the fighting here the most brutal and vicious of the entire Revolution.

By 1779, with certain exceptions such as the infamous Sir Banastre ("Benny") Tarleton, a dashing and peculiarly cruel cavalry officer, British commanders rarely committed deliberate atrocities like those in the 1776 campaign. A lesson had been learned in the North. But American Patriots and Tories, closer to each other, and with a great deal more hatred for each other than Americans and British, indulged in a frenzy of raiding, counterraiding, plundering, and massacre. This fighting took place mostly on the plantations and backcountry farms, between irregulars; sometimes it degenerated into barn burnings and sniping, or bushwhacking, as it was called.

But until the British regulars evacuated the coast, in 1782–1783, the State of Georgia could not be reconstituted. From 1779 onward, it was effectively taken out of the war.

In 1782, shortly before the British departed, Lyman Hall returned. The next year he was elected governor, but he held office only a short time. He retired to private life and died in reduced circumstances in 1790. His only son did not survive him long, and though a Georgia county was named for him, the family disappeared.

George Walton, who had married in 1777, survived wounds, captivity, and wartime service to become chief justice of Georgia in 1783. In 1789 he again was elected governor, and then served in the United States Senate. Walton was remembered by his contemporaries for certain personal traits: like many men who had worked their way upward through great effort he was deeply conservative, tended to despise public opinion and indicated a complete contempt of it when he felt it wrong; he also despised those who started with his own disadvantages but made less effort to help themselves. Walton was always somewhat sensitive about his past, and unlike many of the gentry, who took offices lightly, he would tolerate no slurs on his official posts. He showed enormous respect for merit or talent, wherever found. And from his own background, he had developed a lasting sympathy for young, poor students who came to him for aid. He would do anything for them.

He spent all his professional life in the public service and lived comfortably on his pay. He was relatively poor when he died in 1804. Like Abraham Clark, he was a man of the people, with a morality in some ways ahead of his times.

On December 26, 1779, Sir Henry Clinton sailed with 8,000 British soldiers from New York. Georgia was now firmly under British control, and Clinton left the capable and tough General Wilhelm von Knyphausen in command at New York, with an army matching Washington's. Clinton's grand plan was to keep Washington's Continentals fixed where they were along the Hudson, while he and his lieutenant, General Lord Cornwallis, invaded and conquered the American South.

Clinton's fleet was delayed by winter storms, but he arrived off the Carolina coast near Charleston, in February, 1780. Here the last great campaign, and last great crisis, of the Revolutionary War began.

South of Maryland, especially in the long-settled tidewater regions, there existed more of what was called in the eighteenth century the *aristocratical spirit*. This did not mean there was an established aristocracy in the South; there was not. Life was generally as hard-working and society as open-ended as farther North; it was the state of manners that sometimes deceived. A successful Southerner was expected to be a gentleman, and to live like a gentleman, whatever his origins. The educated groups were definitely expected to show a more refined taste, something frequently scoffed at by more puritan Americans. But in this part of America no class distinctions were fixed by law, except for the institution of Negro slavery which created a bottom caste, outside the effective society.

In the South, local government was increasingly left to the gentry, or *gentlemen of the county*. The gentlemen were not granted this privilege by law, but more by use and wont. Society was just a bit more deferential than in New Jersey. The outlook and ethos of the South forced successful men, even lawyers and medical doctors, to become, or try to become, landed squires on the English model, and this same ethos and example granted them the predominant role in politics. The privilege was not fought for or seized, but handed over by general consent, except among the frontiersmen, whose puritan ethic from Pennsylvania through the Carolinas was much like New England's.

The Southern image irritated many Americans even at the time of the Revolution, at a time when enlightened antislavery sentiment still existed primarily in the South itself. There was always a suspicion that Southerners were planting an aristocracy on the English scale, though actually birth or family counted for no more in Virginia or South Carolina than they did in Delaware or New York, or, to state it more accurately, in all regions landed wealth and family prestige had about equal social weight. The great, frustrated American upper and upper-middle class of the so-called patrician reformers of the nineteenth century were phenomena of the Middle States after the Civil War, when rising concentrations of industrial wealth and immigration destroyed most of the Atlantic gentry's relevance and political power. If the South stayed more static in social terms, through the eighteenth, nineteenth, and twentieth centuries, the lack of industrialization and mixed immigration provides part of the answer. At the time of the Revolution, Northern and Southern democracy were roughly similar; a John Hancock or John Adams was hardly any closer to the average Massachusetts farmer than Thomas Jefferson or Arthur Middleton was to his local "yeomen." It was much later that Northern concepts of democracy changed, while in the South the deferred-to classes themselves were not made irrelevant, but destroyed.

In the eighteenth century, the idea that all powers resided initially in the people, which was English ideology imported from overseas, was held equally in both regions. Virginia was second only to Massachusetts in early rebellion against the Crown, and second to none in the formulation and articulation of basic libertarian credos. The truly surprising thing about men like Washington, Jefferson, Richard Henry Lee, Edward Rutledge, John Adams, Abraham Clark, and George Walton was not that they differed in details, but that they were so much alike, and so much agreed.

Together, they all held an enormous body of *truth to be self-evident*.....

The South Carolinians were closer to England in manners and, in some ways, outlook, than the Puritans and melting-pot products of the North. Significantly, through the background of most prominent leaders of the Revolution in the North runs a family history of rebellion or disaffection in Britain itself. Signer after Signer was descended from a Puritan dissident, or Cromwellian officer, or some type of nonconformist refugee. Their ancestors had not quite blended into the amalgam of organic Anglicanism and Protestant puritanism that ushered in modern England; they represented an ethic that failed in the old country but flowered in the new. But the settlement of the Southern provinces was by a different breed of Englishman, who came more for opportunity than for religious expression. Anglicanism was far stronger in the leading classes in the South, and less resented, than in the Middle Colonies or New England.

Also, cultural connections as well as commercial ties remained. Many great Carolina families regularly returned their sons to England for education; they cultivated both the views and laws of England. Yet a background of local conflict grew in the South, out of conflicting interests and territoriality rather than inherent in the puritan ethic. The notion of civil right was strongly established in seventeenth-century England; the concept of royal prerogative was defeated during the years the colonies were organized. In a sense, Southern Americans were to prove the inherent worth of the English Constitution and English civil liberties by insisting upon them, and to continue effectively the already established English concepts of strong local governments. Probably no other nation could have thrown off colonies so fitted for self-government as Great Britain; no other nation did.

Despite the cultural ties, a steady Americanization took

place in the seventeenth- and early eighteenth-century South. The new American squires, through the assemblies they created out of English history and tradition, soon found themselves battling all forms of prerogative, first that of the Lords Proprietors, then that of the royal executives representing Parliament and the Crown. These struggles generally ended in victories for the colonists. The rights of the Proprietors were surrendered to the Crown. Significantly, many English observers, on the boards of trade or in contact with Americans at the start of the eighteenth century, predicted future trouble and feared an eventual drive for independence. In simple terms, the colonies, North and South, created a new country, and the American refusal to be ruled from abroad, even though they acknowledged British citizenship and sovereignty, was entirely natural and logical, even if not completely understood in its formative years.

Arthur Middleton

The Middleton family of South Carolina provided an example of this process. The first Middleton, Edward, arrived able to sign himself *Gent.* He acquired a large grant of land from the Lords Proprietors. His son, Arthur, was one of the local gentry who turned against the Proprietors and assisted in securing the reversion of their rights. Henry Middleton, the father of the Signer, followed the family tradition of battling against arbitrary executive power; he was a strong supporter of the local legislature and a believer in inherent American rights, and this led to his selection for the First Congress in 1774. He was the Congress' first presiding officer, though he afterward served as President of the South Carolina Provincial Congress and did not return to Philadelphia.

Henry Middleton's oldest son, Arthur, was born and raised at Middleton Place on the Ashley River near Charleston. The family owned approximately fifty thousand acres. Following the custom, young Arthur Middleton was sent "home" for a gentleman's education, first at Hackney, then Westminster and Cambridge. He earned a bachelor's degree, making him one of a tiny educated élite in the English-speaking world. He was admitted to the Middle Temple to read law, which was also a custom of the Southern gentry. Law was taken up not so much as an actual profession but as a preparation for public affairs.

After schooling, Middleton embarked on a two-year Grand Tour of the Continent. He did not get back to Carolina until 1763, when he was twenty-five. He left Europe with the reputation of *profound scholar* and *moral man*.

At this time, it was written that *seats in the assembly were not to be obtained by electioneering arts*—in other words, South Carolina's politics were too deferential in character for demagoguery to achieve office. The son of a prominent father and the scion of an illustrious family, however, was expected to enter public office. Although Middleton had been abroad for a dozen years, his constituency elected him to the assembly in 1764. The same year he married Mary Izard, and was deeded a plantation called Ashley, part of his father's vast holdings.

In the Assembly, Middleton was placed on the committee corresponding with South Carolina's colonial agent in

London. Partially on business and partially on pleasure, since they visited Rome, he and his new wife sailed to England in 1768. The Middletons did not return until 1773, when they settled down at Middleton Place, which had come to Arthur through his mother's inheritance.

Both Henry and Arthur Middleton were now active in the American cause, leaders in an increasingly restive assembly. Both father and son felt a vital constitutional question was at stake, and both also, despite their close English ties and associations, were deeply tinged with a provincial patriotism; this was already a Carolina characteristic. Both attitudes naturally threw them on the American side, although their family connections—Mary Izard Middleton was a cousin of Lady Mary Izard Campbell, wife of Royal Governor Sir William Campbell, who was himself a brother of the Duke of Argyle—might easily have disposed them to be Tories.

The elder Middleton, with Christopher Gadsden, Thomas Lynch, and John and Edward Rutledge, was dispatched to Philadelphia in July, 1774, while Arthur remained in the legislature at home. The assembly was at odds with the governor, part of the historical process that was convulsing the provinces from Massachusetts to Carolina. The Intolerable Acts of 1774 created a hostile atmosphere in early 1775. The assembly, called the Provincial Congress, petitioned Sir William Campbell with a list of American grievances. The protest shocked and irritated actually, he was allowed no latitude by the Ministry to Campbell; he refused flatly to receive or discuss it; and treat with colonials on these issues. But Sir William had a crafty streak: he showed himself friendly, if cool, in order not to arouse more opposition. He expected trouble, and he had written for British troops; he hoped to delay a break until they arrived. When the troops debarked at Charleston, Campbell hinted darkly, to close associates, then he would put down these *new-fangled authorities of the day*—this planters' Congress, which apparently believed it should govern Carolina.

He spoke a bit too openly in the tangled maze of conflicting ideological, family, and factional loyalties that was developing at Charleston. One of his confidants, with strong local loyalties, betrayed the secret to the patriot Congress. The Provincial Congress appointed a secret committee of five, one of whom was Arthur Middleton, in April, 1775. This committee's mission was to place the colony in a posture of defense against the royal government. It took quick action, creating a militia and seizing the royal magazines and all munitions in the public armories. The secret committee (C. C. Pinckney was another member) was far advanced in promoting resistance in the South at this time.

The real crisis came in June. Sir William Campbell, still expecting reinforcements, kept dissembling. He was courteous to the rebellious party, but sent word to *friends of the royal government* in the province, including backwoods Tories and Indians, to be ready to act at a later date. This communication was also betrayed, and it prompted Arthur Middleton to demand that Campbell be arrested in the name of the Colony.

The matter was debated, but a majority hesitated to take such bold action. Religious, commercial, and military ties were mentioned in rebuttal; few Carolinians actually wanted a war with the British Empire. The motion failed. Word of the discussion, however, reached Campbell and so frightened him that he deserted Charleston for the safety of a British sloop. Here he worked more to get British intervention than to support the local Loyalists. Campbell had a personal interest not common to royal governors—his wife held large properties in the colony.

South Carolina began to reorganize its local government, but at first with no serious intent of permanent rupture. Significantly, the colony refused to join in the Nonexportation Acts of the First Congress until rice was removed from the items prohibited for export to England. The colony lived off the export of rice and indigo, and it was further recorded that the compromise on one crop, but not the other, infuriated the indigo planters. All through 1775–1776 the local struggles at Charleston tended to dominate, and South Carolina's leadership paid less attention than some colonials to the Continental Congresses. The more toward full rebellion and independence was pushed over great opposition by a small group of influential men, notably Christopher Gadsden and John Drayton. It was noticeable that admitted patriots such as the Middletons and the Rutledge brothers, John and Edward, wavered back and forth on the ultimate issue, now "violent," now moderate.

The same delegation from the colony was returned to Philadelphia in May, 1775. Thomas Lynch and Gadsden supported John Adams' moves toward fighting a *full war* and thus moved closer to the idea of full independence; Henry Middleton was reserved and noncommittal; Edward Rutledge seemed to go from heated opposition to the British to a position of moderation leader. Some light on the local sentiment at Charleston is thrown by an event on Gadsden's return in January, 1776 to accept a colonelcy of a militia regiment.

Gadsden brought back a copy of *Common Sense* and a flaming conviction never to submit to Parliament. In a speech in the Provincial Congress approving South Carolina's new government, he expressed himself in favor of *absolute* independence. This revelation was badly received by a majority; even those who thought with Gadsden said he had been imprudent in suddenly broaching it to an unprepared assembly.

Shortly afterward, the Provincial Congress reëlected Henry Middleton, Thomas Lynch, and John and Edward Rutledge to the Continental body. John Rutledge asked that his name be withdrawn. It was not, but he stayed at home, since he was also elected provisional governor of the colony. Henry Middleton, who had done much to prepare the new government and lead it to acceptance, begged to be excused from the long trip north because of *infirmities of age*. The Congress obliged him by nominating his son Arthur in his place. Gadsden, because of his *imprudent* mention of independence, was dropped; he was replaced by Thomas Heyward, Junior. Then, when the Carolina Congress heard that Thomas Lynch was stricken with apoplexy at Philadelphia, and Thomas, Junior, desired to attend him, it gave young Lynch full credentials as a sixth delegate.

This delegation was given wide discretion, but not specifically empowered to opt for independence. Opinion in South Carolina continued very mixed. The new government was not officially "rebel"; it was rationalized as a temporary measure until *differences were resolved*. But John Drayton, the new chief justice, on April 23, 1776, in charging a grand jury, declared George III had abdicated the government: *he has no authority over us, and we owe no obedience to him. . . . The Almighty created*

America to be independent of Britain; to refuse our labors
in this divine work, is to refuse to be a great, a free, a
pious, and a happy people! Apparently, most South Carolinians did not really expect to be reunited with Great
Britain, though there was great concern for reëstablishing
the commercial ties under new management.

The four South Carolina delegates who remained in the
Continental Congress reflected this state of mind into the
summer of 1776. Because of the state of Carolina politics
they were something of a "second team." Edward Rutledge
was less famous than his brother, John. Middleton and
Lynch were sons of prominent fathers who owed their appointments to family prestige, and Thomas Heyward, Jr.,
also was distinguished more by family than actual achieve-
ment. They were considered reliable young men by the
Provincial Congress, capable of handling a secondary front.
Middleton, at thirty-three, was the oldest; the others were
still in their twenties. Edward Rutledge was elected to the
First Congress at twenty-four, and he was the youngest
Signer at twenty-six. Strikingly, these four were men of the
same generation and class, all educated in England, and
all quite rich.

Edward Rutledge/.

Edward Rutledge was born in or near Charleston, the
youngest son of an Irish doctor and Sarah Hext, a Charleston heiress of some fortune. Sarah Hext Rutledge was wid-
owed at twenty-seven, with seven children. She was able to
afford them splendid educations.

Edward, Hugh, and John Rutledge were trained in the classics, then entered the Middle Temple in London in preparation for the law. John became the most distinguished barrister in the province, Hugh, a prominent jurist. Edward followed in their footsteps, coming back from England in 1773 to begin the practice of law. He married Henrietta Middleton, Arthur's sister, in March, 1774, and in July of that year was selected with, and probably on account of, his brother John for a seat in the First Congress.

[signature: Thomas Heyward Junr.]

Thomas Heyward, Jr., was the son of Colonel Daniel Heyward of "Old House," Granville County, a self-made but extremely wealthy planter. The elder Heyward insisted upon a gentleman's education for his son: a classical education, followed up by a period at the Inns of Court, Temple Bar. Young Heyward made the Grand Tour and returned in the same year as Middleton and Rutledge, 1773. Expressing a strong preference for the American position, Heyward was elected to the newly organized Provincial Assembly in 1775. He was handsome and popular, with *most amiable manners*. He served on the Committee of Safety before he was dispatched to replace Colonel Christopher Gadsden in the Second Congress.

According to one biographer, Heyward modestly declined this appointment, until a large group of older, more distinguished Carolinians personally called upon him and urged him to serve. He showed no real taste for Congressional service.

Thomas Lynch Jun

The fourth South Carolina delegate was also pushed into office, somewhat against his will. Thomas Lynch, Jr., was of remote Austrian descent (the family name was originally Linz) out of Ireland; one Jonack Lynch emigrated from Connaught late in the seventeenth century. Jonack Lynch discovered how to grow rice profitably on the rich alluvial soils along the North and South Santee; he avoided the feverish swamps which had been the rice belt until his time. His discovery allowed him to build a princely estate.

Jonack's son Thomas Lynch, Sr., was a planter of great fortune, reputation, and influence, who served almost continuously in the South Carolina Assembly. He sent his son through Eton and Cambridge, and urged him to enroll at Temple Bar. Thomas Junior, who showed an indolent disposition, never finished his legal studies, returning home in 1772. It was reported that while in England, he had found friends among several highly-placed Whig families, who inflamed his dislike of the Tory ascendancy under George III.

The elder Lynch deeded his son the plantation of Peach Tree on the North Santee when he married a childhood sweetheart, Elizabeth Shubrick. Lynch Sr. gave him his blessing to enter public life; one of the more concise biographies of the younger Lynch states that *his family got him office.*

In 1774–1775 both Lynches were arrayed on the planter, or rebel side against the royal government. Thomas Senior, a respected member of the Provincial Congress, went to Philadelphia. Young Thomas was appointed a captain in the First South Carolina Regiment. His father at first urged him to decline in the hope of higher rank, and to join him at Philadelphia. But Lynch refused to do this, and embarked on arduous service. With a fellow company commander, Charles C. Pinckney, he marched on a recruiting sweep through North Carolina in 1775. The drive was successful, but Lynch contracted "swamp fever" which destroyed his health. He had never been strong, and he arrived back at Charleston barely able to walk.

When, in 1776, he heard that his father had suffered a stroke, he applied to Colonel Gadsden for leave. Gadsden, noted for his Roman sense of duty as well as his views for independence, refused. The gesture of the Provincial Congress in appointing Lynch to the Philadelphia meeting unanimously was probably both a sentimental gesture and a slap at the outspoken colonel as well.

Lynch arrived in Philadelphia almost incapacitated; he was not to make much of a mark.

In this young group Edward Rutledge was the acknowledged leader. John Adams' various mentions of him are somewhat ironic. On their first meeting, Ned Rutledge remarked that the King's promises were worthless, and this caused Adams to write in his diary: *This is a young, smart, spirited body.*

But when the younger Rutledge made it evident he distrusted the "violent party" and engaged Adams in *nibbling and quibbling*, the diary recorded: *Young Ned Rutledge is a perfect Bob-o-Lincoln—a swallow, a sparrow, a peacock. . . .*

Under Rutledge's leadership, the South Carolinians moved solidly into the moderate, or dilatory corner. Their stands show clearly that they did not favor reconciliation with Britain to the extent the Pennsylvanians did, but simply opposed the declaration of independence. Their actions also indicate that they expected little support for a declaration at home. Adams meanwhile wrote his personal diatribes. *Rutledge is a very uncouth and ungraceful speaker . . . tedious upon frivolous points.*

Benjamin Rush's comment is probably much more fair: *A sensible young lawyer, of great volubility in speaking, and very useful in the business of Congress.* Rutledge was indeed *frivolous on tedious points*; it was the principal way in which he could impede Adams' rush toward independence, and he delayed, put off, and frustrated Adams', Lee's, and Jefferson's designs with considerable parliamentary skill.

Adams also accused Rutledge, Lynch, and Arthur Middleton of being subverted socially by the *proprietary gentlemen* of Pennsylvania, since they attended many parties thrown by the Loyalist-leaning elements. Henrietta Middleton Rutledge came to Philadelphia, and truthfully, the wealthy, amiable, and Anglican young planters appeared birds of brilliant but dubious plumage to the New Englanders. On the other hand, John Hancock, also noted for his exquisite dress, got along very well with them.

During the crucial debates, Adams wrote of Arthur Middleton that he . . . *became the hero of the Quaker and proprietary politics in Congress. He had little information and less argument; in rudeness and sarcasm his forte lay, and he played off his artillery without reserve.* But Adams' *Autobiography* also says the two parted without *a spark of malice on either side; for he was an honest and generous fellow, with all his zeal in this cause.*

Rush described the younger Middleton as a *man of cynical temper, but of upright intentions towards his country. . . . he disliked business, and when put upon the Committee of Accounts he refused to serve and gave as a reason for it that he hated accounts, that he did not even keep his own accounts, and that he knew nothing about them.*

There must remain a very strong suspicion that the elegant indolence assumed by the Southerners, and their "aristocratical" protrayal of manners made these beautifully-dressed, English-educated youngsters appear something of popinjays to other men who wanted to get something done, specifically a declaration.

The South Carolina Congressmen, or delegates, were given enormous latitude in the absence of formalized political parties. They were expected to serve the interests of their region, but to follow their own conscience in the crunch. Rutledge did this. On the moderate side in June, 1776, he and three others sustained the *whole Argument,* and his motion to put off the final vote for the Declaration was right in his *own Eyes.* The Carolinians were for all the other acts of Congress, but saw *no Wisdom* in baldly asserting independence.

On July 1, 1776, the Lee resolution carried the colonies as a whole, nine to two. South Carolina and Pennsylvania were opposed, with Delaware deadlocked and New York abstaining. Rutledge then requested the final vote to be put over one more day, hinting that South Carolina would join the majority.

The Carolina delegates did this on July 2, not changing

173

their minds, but agreeing that the American cause would be hurt by a lack of unanimity. The four young men signed the Declaration the next month without protest.

The delegation had played a prominent and influential part at Philadelphia. Like certain of the gentlemen from New York, Rutledge was a Whig and a patriot, but also a leader who *detested the ascendancy of the mob*. He did not desire a national independence that might allow a popular, direct government. On this subject he was a vehement, and certainly one of the ablest, spokesmen of his section and his class. He acceded to the majority on July 2 as a graceful and basically a patriotic gesture. On another matter of great historic importance, Rutledge was entirely successful, for better or for worse. Although he personally, along with a large number of enlightened planters considered Negro slavery an evil and even voted for a ban on importation, he also realized the tremendous economic problem posed by the South's half-million slaves. Rutledge was instrumental in getting Jefferson's references to slavery stricken from the Declaration—he made this the final price of South Carolina's solidarity.

Rutledge, Middleton, and the others sent the Declaration south with some trepidation—but meanwhile, events of which they knew nothing had occurred. In June, 1776, a British fleet under Sir Peter Parker landed soldiers commanded by Sir Henry Clinton near Charleston in an attempt to seize the port. But a gallant defense of the harbor by General William Moultrie frustrated the operation. The earlier action of training militia, seizing the British munitions and cannon, and recruiting men in North Carolina all paid dividends. In this action Sir William Campbell, who courageously landed with the troops, was wounded.

The repulse saved Charleston from occupation for four more years. It also created a climate of victorious euphoria in which the Declaration, when it arrived, was hailed on August 5, 1776, with prayers and thunderous cheers.

Thomas Lynch's father died soon after he signed, and Lynch retired from public life, resigning his seat in Congress. His health by now was very poor. Rush said of him: *A man of moderate talents and timid in difficult circumstances of his country.* This is not flattering, but unquestionably basically true. Lynch never wanted to be a lawyer, nor a public servant, a soldier, nor a delegate to Congress. Circumstances—and a dominant father—forced him into each career. The war, with the fever he caught on service, also killed him. He lived on in illness on his plantation until 1779, then, on medical advice, sought a change of climate. He and his young wife took ship for the neutral Dutch island of Saint Eustatius in the fall of 1779. The ship and all its passengers disappeared in a storm at sea.

The other three Signers saw distinguished service in the Revolution. They were of military age, and all took commissions in the South Carolina state forces. Heyward and Rutledge served as officers of the Charleston Ancient Battalion of Artillery. While in the militia, Middleton was elected governor of the state, but he declined the office, which then passed to John Rutledge.

All three were in Charleston when Sir Henry Clinton made his second, successful assault on the city in March, 1780. The earlier fortifications unfortunately had been allowed to fall into disrepair; the city was unprotected from the sea. General Benjamin Lincoln, the American commander, was badly outnumbered by the British. Lincoln, from the purely military aspect, should not have attempted to defend. But, as in Washington's decision to defend New York in 1776, politics forced his hand. Charleston, with twelve thousand inhabitants, was the most important center in the South; the political effect of surrendering so many citizens without a fight was considered disastrous. Lincoln hesitated, while the British threw strong forces around the city; he was trapped, besieged, and lost. After forty days of siege, under vicious bombardment, at the end, which destroyed civilian morale, Lincoln capitulated.

Clinton captured six thousand Continentals and armed militia, three hundred cannon, and five ships with seven general officers, including Lincoln. It was the greatest single American disaster of the war. A few days after this victory, the British, under Tarleton, trapped another four hundred Continentals under Buford near the North Carolina line. This force, composed mainly of Virginians, was massacred, after attempting to surrender. With this last defeat, formal resistance to the invaders collapsed in South Carolina.

During the siege of Charleston, Thomas Heyward served as a judge of the newly independent Criminal and Civil Court. His close friends urged him not to take this post, since it was thankless, of lower rank than Congressman, and might make him a marked man. But Heyward accepted the unpleasant duty of presiding over the trial of several Tories. When these men were adjudged guilty of treason, Heyward saw to it they were hanged. This marked him for special Tory reprisal.

The three Signers were captured with the troops in Charleston. Heyward was wounded in action during the last days of the siege. General Lincoln requested Edward

Rutledge to try to break out through enemy lines, but Rutledge did not go. He believed he should stay and share the common fate. Arthur Middleton continued to fight even after Middleton Place, along with his wife and children, was taken over by the British in the tightening siege.

The Middleton family seat was despoiled, though not burned. The splendid collection of paintings was slashed with sabers. The slaves, silver, and furnishings were taken away. A British historian admitted, *There was much private emolument, which added no lustre to British arms.* Arthur Middleton's loss was immense. Two hundred of his slaves were sold off to plantations in the British West Indies, and all his lands sequestered by the Crown. Mary Izard Middleton, with her husband in captivity and all his lands confiscated, was without money to sustain her children. She had to humiliate herself by appearing before the British commissioner in Charleston to beg the return of some personal property. She was treated fairly, and allowed some revenues, only because some of the Izard family were Loyalists. The favor was repaid, in a sense, when, in 1782, a convicted Tory was released by the patriots because of his family connections to the Middletons, who had suffered so much.

With the permission of the British authorities, Tories occupied the Heyward plantations. Thomas Heyward's mansion, "White Hall," was plundered, his lands devastated, and the fields burned. One hundred and thirty slaves were carried off. These unfortunates, like those taken from Middleton, were not freed, but sold south in Jamaica, apparently at some personal profit to the looters. Heyward had two younger brothers. These boys were not imprisoned or molested because they were still minors, though this leniency was bitterly protested by Charleston's Tories, who never forgave Heyward's judicial executions of Tories.

Edward Rutledge's kin did not escape. The family properties were raided and sequestered. His mother, Sarah Hext Rutledge, was considered dangerous to the Crown. She was arrested, removed from her plantation home, and confined in Charleston. Through all this she maintained a stout defiance of the British.

After the victory on the coast, the invading army established posts throughout South Carolina. They reconstituted the royal government and seemed to have brought the province back within the Empire. But the pacification was more apparent than real. The British controlled only the ground on which their military camps stood, and the Tories they relied on so heavily were unable to sway the bulk of the people back to the King. Guerrilla warfare erupted as it had in Georgia. Francis Marion, Andrew Pickens, and Thomas Sumter, all men with a certain genius for irregular warfare, kept rebellion alive. They struck out of the swamps and backwoods, hitting British posts and punishing Tory collaborators. There were bushwacking and hit-and-run raids on both sides, as Loyalists and patriots engaged in a civil war which the occupying British could not control. Houses were burned, men were shot down, and women, children, and many hapless slaves were driven into the swamps to die. This Southern campaign exceeded the Northern operations in brutality and viciousness. All contemporary accounts, and most historians, agree that South Carolina, with Georgia, suffered the greatest devastation and bloodshed during the American Revolution.

Rutledge, Heyward, and Middleton—who was noted for a high temper—remained cool and steady at this turn of fortune. All were offered the *protection of the Crown,* or amnesty, if they would change their coats; all refused. They also refused exchange. They were shipped out to the British stockade at St. Augustine, Florida, where the most dangerous prisoners and incorrigibles were kept. Here they suffered a number of indignities and privations; for a time the British commandant was undecided whether to treat them as civil criminals or as prisoners of war. In either category, their condition was hard.

Heyward, who had some poetic skill, defied the guards by writing new words to "God Save the King"; he taught the American prisoners to sing a ballad called "God Save the States" to the old tune, and this hardly improved his treatment. While he was imprisoned in Florida, his young wife died at home.

The three were finally exchanged in late 1781, in a general exchange of prisoners between the Crown and Congress. Heyward and Rutledge were members of the patriot legislature that convened at Jacksonborough in 1782, while Middleton was reappointed to Congress by John Rutledge, the governor. At the end of the war all returned to find general devastation, but their lands remained and they were held in high honor.

Heyward continued as a judge. Middleton and Rutledge remained active in state politics, and they were instrumental in seeing that the civil law was reëstablished firmly and equitably in ravaged South Carolina. After the bitterness of the civil strife and occupation, there was a widespread clamor to confiscate the property not only of Tories, but also of all who had done business in any way with the British, and to repudiate all private, civil debt. Middleton and Rutledge, despite their losses, were adamant in opposition, and their influence helped uphold the law and kept the state from further social and class conflict. Rutledge also drafted the law which abolished primogeniture.

Middleton died soon after the war, but Rutledge continued a long and eminent career as a lawyer and state legislator. When he died in 1800, he was one of the state's greatest citizens. He was given a splendid funeral oration, and a monument was erected at Charleston to his memory.

Through 1780, the war was going badly for the American cause in the South. South Carolina and Georgia were reoccupied, and if not entirely pacified, taken out of the conflict. Washington, who with the main Continental army was still facing General Knyphausen at New York, was gravely concerned. He wanted to send the man he considered his best general, Nathanael Greene, to the Southern Department to assume command. The Congress, however, insisted that the elderly Horatio Gates, the victor of Saratoga, be appointed. Gates had retired to a farm in Virginia, but he accepted the command and rode south into North Carolina. Here he took command of approximately 1,000 veteran Delaware and Maryland Continentals, whom he found desperately short of supply.

The North Carolina militia, or state troops, had mustered, but there was rivalry between them and the Continentals, who were being treated almost as foreign soldiers in the state. North Carolina supplied its own men, but lagged in feeding the regulars. To solve this problem, Horatio Gates "joined" the Continentals to the North Carolina militia. On August 14, 1780, he marched into South Carolina with 3,000 troops, two-thirds of whom were raw militia. He moved against Camden, where Francis, Lord Rawdon had positioned some 1,300 British regulars.

Meanwhile, Sir Henry Clinton, feeling South Carolina was under control, had decided to return to New York. He left his second in command, Lieutenant General Charles Earl Cornwallis in charge in the South. He gave Cornwallis strict orders not to endanger British control of South Carolina by extensive operations north of the state line. Before Clinton departed, he and Cornwallis quarreled over strategy.

Cornwallis was in Charleston when he heard news of Gate's march. He took 900 British troops and rushed toward Camden to join Rawdon and assume overall command. His force bumped into the American army near Camden during the night of August 15. Unable to see or maneuver in the dark, both forces recoiled to wait for daylight.

General Gates's troops were largely untrained, and all were suffering from dysentery caused by inadequate diet. His principal officers urged a retreat, but Gates decided to offer battle. Purely by chance, he now placed his least reliable militia units opposite Cornwallis' sturdiest regular infantry in forming the order of battle.

When the battle was joined, these units collapsed in the face of a British attack. The Continentals, at the other end of the line, pushed Lord Rawdon's contingent back, only to find themselves struck in the flank when Cornwallis' victorious regiments wheeled from pursuing the fleeing militia. Although these men, and their commander, "Baron" de Kalb, fought gallantly against overwhelming odds, they were totally defeated. Johann de Kalb was killed, and at least 750 Americans were killed or captured.

Gates left the field and galloped toward Virginia, and again went into retirement. In one hour he had destroyed all the prestige gained at Saratoga. Daniel Morgan of Virginia took over the American stragglers in North Carolina. Then, three days after the disaster at Camden, Tarleton's cavalry surrounded and surprised Sumter's guerrilla force and wiped it out.

The American cause in the South seemed doomed.

But Cornwallis' success caused dangerous overconfidence in the British commander. The prospect of seizing North Carolina was irrestistible. He now disregarded Clinton's orders and started toward Charlotte with his main force. A body of about 1,000 Tories, under Patrick Ferguson, was detached to sweep up through the southwest, devastate the backcountry, and join Cornwallis on the coast. The war now came to North Carolina.

Joseph Hewes,

North Carolina was originally settled as a part of Proprietary South Carolina; until 1711, the two Carolinas were one. North Carolina succeeded in becoming a royal province in 1729. Its settlement lagged behind its neighbors to the south and north, and, as in Georgia, many of its people entered from other American colonies. None of North Carolina's Signers was native-born: two came from the North, and one from Virginia.

One from New Jersey, Joseph Hewes, played a key role in the Declaration of Independence. John Adams once wrote to Thomas Jefferson: . . . *and you know that the unanimity of the States finally depended upon the vote of Joseph Hewes, and was finally determined by him.*

Hewes' parents, Aaron and Providence, were Friends. The family had originally settled along the Connecticut-Massachusetts frontier, but moved to New Jersey due to Indian troubles and the persecution of the Society of Friends that was common in the New England of those years. New England and the South then had established churches; the Middle Colonies, which were polyglot, consequently drew large concentrations of Baptists, Mennonites, Quakers, Lutherans, and Presbyterians. Joseph Hewes was born at Kingston, New Jersey, in 1730 and raised as a member of the Society.

After schooling, Hewes was apprenticed to a counting house in Philadelphia. He then became a successful merchant on his own. Seeking new opportunity, he transferred his operations south, to Edenton, North Carolina, apparently prior to 1763. Here, he established a mercantile business with his nephew, Nathaniel Allen.

Hewes, whom Rush described as, *A plain, worthy merchant, and well acquainted with business,* was soon highly regarded in his new setting. He became a patron of the town, and enjoyed an enviable reputation among its leading citizens. By 1766 he was elected to sit in the Provincial Assembly as a borough member. In this post he took a public position that the acts of Parliament were *impolitic, unjust, and cruel, as well as unconstitutional and destructive of American rights.* With Richard Caswell and William Hooper, he was asked to represent North Carolina in the First Congress in 1774. At Philadelphia, he was a supporter of the non-importation agreement, although his own business was importing. Hewes' own words indicate his beliefs: *We want no revolution. But every American to a man is determined to die or be free.* By taking this stand, Hewes risked his role business and his entire fortune, which consisted of waterfront lots, wharves, and warehouses devoted to British commerce.

Hewes suffered two personal tragedies. He was engaged to Isabella Johnston, sister of the President of the North Carolina Assembly. She died a few days before the day set for the wedding, and Hewes never married. He was also Quaker, with a long Quaker, pacifist heritage. The majority of the large, prosperous Quaker communities of New Jersey and Pennsylvania refused to support the Continental Congresses, fearing resistance would lead to war. Hewes took the position that liberty was too important to be surrendered from a reluctance to resist tyranny by force. When the Quaker Meeting of Philadelphia denounced the Congress for its war moves, Hewes broke with it and never attended another Meeting.

He was cited by Rush, Adams, and others for his efficient work in committees. With his knowledge of shipping, he was put on the Marine Committee. More than any other man, he was responsible for fitting out the first American navy. Hewes had met a sea captain named John Paul Jones and developed a deep respect for him. He personally secured the ship on which Jones eventually sailed; thus a Quaker gave America its first naval hero.

Although North Carolina, in April, 1776, became the first British colony to instruct its Continental delegation to *concur with the Delegates of the other colonies in declaring Independency,* Joseph Hewes remained personally dubious of the act. When Richard Henry Lee's June 7 motion came up before the house, he was the only delegate from his province; the other two, William Hooper and John Penn, had gone home for an important session of the Provincial Congress.

As John Adams, who was desperately pushing independence, wrote later, *The measure had been on the market for months, and obstinately opposed from day to day.* The colonies stood six and six—for and opposed, without North Carolina. Hewes stubbornly cast his vote with the moderates. *For many days the majority depended on Mr. Hewes, of North Carolina.*

Hewes searched his conscience, and suddenly changed his vote. Adams described the scene: *Mr. Hewes, who had hitherto constantly voted against it, started upright, and lifting up both hands to Heaven . . . cried out, "It is done! and I will abide by it."* Adams went on to describe the consternation on the faces of the old moderate majority as Hewes threw a new majority of one to independence. Only Rutledge's immediate motion of adjournment postponed the matter until July.

Hewes did, indeed, abide by his decision. With John Penn, who favored the motion, he voted for it on July 1 and 2. He then buried himself in committee work, and at one time supplied gunpowder to the army at his own expense. He awed his colleagues by his determination to work; he was at his desk twelve hours a day, often without pausing to eat. Hewes wrote in a letter, *My country is entitled to my services, and I shall not shrink from her cause, even though it should cost me my life.*

Hewes' health was poor before he signed the Declaration, and his death, in 1779, was due to overwork in Congress. Hewes died in Philadelphia at fifty, a lonely man, unmarried and apart from his community of Friends. He was buried in the cemetery of Christ Church, where Benjamin Franklin, Robert Morris, and Francis Hopkinson rented pews.

Wm Hooper

William Hooper, though a member of Congress, did not arrive at Philadelphia for the July voting. He was another transplanted Yankee, born in Boston, where his father was rector of Trinity Church. He had graduated from Harvard in 1760, and studied law under James Otis, whose startling *Rights of the British Colonies Asserted and Proved* of 1764 was the first American rebuttal to the British North America Proclamation of 1763. This background permitted him later to become close, even intimate, with John Adams in later years. Although his family were to be Tories, William Hooper turned Whig soon after college. Undoubtedly, he absorbed many of Otis' ideas.

He also found Boston somewhat overcrowded with lawyers. After corresponding with some New England migrants in the South, he took ship for Wilmington, North Carolina, in 1764. Contemporary writings describe Wilmington as a *liberal and congenial* town, and Hooper as a handsome, graceful, well-spoken young man. He entered into the practice of law, and soon was something of a favorite of the leading attorneys and planters of the Cape Fear community. In 1767 he married Anne Clark, the daughter of an old Carolina family, and this marriage made him entirely acceptable in the highest North Carolina social and political circles. The Bostonian moved in high company. Two successive royal governors went out of their way to cultivate him as a coming man of influence, and the chief justice of the province entertained him frequently in his home.

Hooper became deputy attorney-general of the province. This led to his siding strongly with the Governor's Party against the Carolina Regulators in 1771.

North Carolina, like Pennsylvania, had a large Scots-Irish Appalachian frontier community. The same east-west struggle developed between the established, conservative tidewater and the rawer, more democratic-minded foot-hills. The east dominated the Assembly, the courts, and wrote the local laws, many of which, on finance, taxation, and representation, the backwoodsmen felt were discriminatory or unfair. A group rose in the western counties called the Regulators. The Regulators included both honest farmers with grievances as well as leaders who attacked the whole social order of the colony. When bloodshed ensued between Regulators and eastern-controlled sheriffs, Hooper entered the conflict entirely on the side of the eastern planters and the Crown, who were at this time allied. He urged the strongest measures against the westerners, and the tidewater militia put them down.

William Hooper, who was considered charming among his own circle, tended to be cool, aloof, and courageous toward the common people, a cultivated lawyer who *viewed the crowd coldly.* He was then and later appalled by some of the patriots who linked resistance to the Crown with popular democracy; he never became any sort of popular leader. When he was first elected to the North Carolina Assembly, in 1773, he immediately became leader of the Whig faction. There was no inconsistency in this stand.

Hooper fought the Parliamentary acts, and especially the Attachment Bill, a rider which made courts and magistrates dependent solely on revenues from the Crown. Hitherto, these had been supported by local assessments voted by the various legislatures; the net effect of the rider, which was opposed by almost the entire American legal profession, was to put courts and judges beyond effective colonial influence. Hooper believed this was not only unjust, but unconstitutional.

Under his leadership, the North Carolina legislature voted down the bill, with the result that all courts were suspended for a year. This struck at Hooper's own income—without courts, there was no practice of law. Because of this stand, Hooper was sent to the First Congress by the Assembly in 1774.

Most of Anne Clark Hooper's relations were Loyalists, and many of Hooper's friends had a Tory bent. He rapidly became repugnant to them. There were attempts to intimidate him when he joined the Committee of Correspondence and argued for the relief of Boston.

In the Congress, Rush considered him *a sensible, sprightly lawyer, and a rapid, but correct speaker.* Adams praised him as one of the best orators in the house, although Hooper took a conciliatory position toward all Loyalists. In March, 1776, he wrote Governor Johnston that most of all he wanted *peace and reconciliation,* but only on honorable terms; he would submit to no others. When the Provincial Congress authorized independence, Hooper accepted this, and signed the Declaration willingly.

While he was in Congress he moved his family out of Wilmington to an estate called "Finian" on Masonboro Sound; he believed they would be safer on Cape Fear than in the town. During his absence, however, a British sloop of war sailed by the estate and fired several cannon balls at Hooper's house.

Hooper stayed in Congress until 1777, serving on many committees. During his public service, he had depleted his private finances, and in April, 1777, he returned to the practice of law. But he was made the subject of a man-hunt by the patrolling British. On one occasion a warship landed a party under a field officer, which beat the bushes for him; he narrowly escaped.

When the British moved into North Carolina in 1780, Hooper was in an agony of concern and indecision about his wife and children. The hideous, bushwhacking warfare of South Carolina was feared on the Cape. Finally, he sent his family into Wilmington, believing they would be safer in the custody of the British Army than exposed to Tory reprisal. They were safe, but this decision caused him great distress, because he was separated from them for many months. Hooper himself fled to the interior of the state, where he caught malaria.

The property he left behind was deliberately destroyed, as he had feared.

The end of the Revolution found Hooper sick and ruined financially. He was one of those patriots who never recovered what he lost through public service. He moved away from Wilmington, and died in 1790.

John Penn

The third North Carolina Signer, John Penn, had a career similar to that of George Walton of Georgia, although Penn was born in better circumstances. His Virginian father left him a comfortable estate, but Penn still suffered, as he said, *from a striking deficiency of parental attention.* The elder Penn did not believe in education, and he made no effort to see that his son obtained one. At eighteen, John Penn had only about two years of country schooling, hardly enough for literacy.

When Moses Penn died, John realized his deficiencies; the day when a planter who could barely sign his name could make a place for himself in society was long past in America. Penn humbly presented himself to a kinsman, Edmund Pendleton, Esquire, who was one of the most distinguished lawyers and citizens of Virginia. Pendleton commented that it was late for a grown man to start school—in that era most men who sought an education had graduated from college by eighteen. But Pendleton agreed to help and opened up his splendid library to the youth.

A few years later, Penn was licensed to practice law in Virginia. He was apparently an effective pleader at the bar, for he was *frequently known to draw tears from both the court and jury.*

He practiced in Virginia for a dozen years. Many of his friends and relations had moved to North Carolina; in 1774 he joined them, moving his wife and family to Granville County. Penn had an attractive personality and was already an established lawyer. He quickly became a leader in his new community. In 1775 North Carolina sent him to the Continental Congress, as well as to the Provincial Congress at Halifax. Penn had the strong Whig views of Edmund Pendleton and a majority of the Virginia planter group. From Congress he wrote back: *My first wish is that America may be free; the second that we may be restored to peace. . . .*

He was one of the first to see that seeking foreign aid for the Revolution meant a final separation from Great Britain. By early 1776 he had lost hope that there would be any conciliation with the mother country.

Dr. Rush remembered him as a *good humored man, very talkative in company, but seldom spoke in Congress. . . . He was honest, and warmly attached to the liberties of his country.*

Penn's Congressional service between 1775 and 1779 came at enormous personal sacrifice: his law practice dissolved and his income dried up. He enjoyed the reputation of hard worker, both in Congress and in his state. When the British moved into North Carolina in the fall of 1780, John Penn was appointed to the state Board of War.

This was a time of terror in the state. Cornwallis sent dozens of Tory agents ahead, with orders to locate and turn out the Loyalists, take up arms, and turn out the patriot government. The regular militia had been shattered with Gates at Camden. While there were never nearly so many Tories as Cornwallis hoped, many North Carolinians now believed their only recourse was to take the "King's Protection," or else court exile and ruin.

John Penn and the Board of War made tremendous efforts to raise a defense. Penn was given gubernatorial, even dictatorial powers, by the frightened Assembly. He sent out appeal after appeal for the farmers to assembly under arms to protect their homes and families. Horsemen rode through the backcountry, in the path of Major Patrick Ferguson's feared Tory Rangers, to rouse the region. Penn wrote, *For God's sake, . . . encourage our People, animate them to dare even to die for their Country!*

As Ferguson's horde swept north across the state line, hundreds of tough, rifle-toting frontiersmen turned out. John Sevier and Isaac Shelby walked in from across the mountains, from what was then part of North Carolina but is now Tennessee. They joined forces with William Campbell and some Virginia backwoodsmen, and with the North Carolina militia under Benjamin Cleveland, Charles McDowell, and James Williams, in the corner where modern Virginia, North Carolina, and Tennessee meet. These men were not tidewater militia, commanded by gentlemen; they were veterans of the Indian wars, hard, grim, determined, and dangerous. They despised Tories.

Ferguson, one of the few British officers who understood American combat, scented danger and moved back into South Carolina. The American force followed him. He chose to fight at Kings Mountain, a long, steep hill not far inside the South Carolina border. The American frontiersmen attacked him on the night of October 7, 1780. The result was a vicious battle and Tory massacre: *bodies of Tories were lying all over the mountain,* as one participant wrote. Ferguson and 225 of his men were killed; more than 150 were wounded; and 100 surrendered. The total patriot casualties were less than 100 killed and wounded.

The frontiersmen hung nine of the prisoners, who were accused of specific crimes, by torchlight. Then, the "overmountain men" went home. The North Carolina militia marched the prisoners north. The news of this tremendous defeat reached Lord Cornwallis at Charlotte and so unnerved him he abandoned the conquest of North Carolina and hurried south again.

At the end of the crisis, John Penn, who had worked coolly, courageously, and effectively through the worst days, surrendered his office and his powers. He returned to the practice of law. He was never to regain his former affluence and standing. He had sacrificed everything in the public service, and he died in obscurity in 1788.

Rays of Ligh

In the years and months before Lexington and Concord, the two colonies of Massachusetts and Virginia kept pace with each other and led all the others along the road to rebellion. In this struggle in the Old Dominion no one was more prominent or more effective than Richard Henry Lee.

Richard Henry Lee

The Lees were a distinguished American family long before 1776. The great-grandfather of Richard Henry Lee had secured nominal dominion status for the Colony of Virginia from Oliver Cromwell; he had also persuaded the royal governor, Sir William Berkeley, to declare Virginia an integral part of the King's dominions while Charles II was in exile. These seventeenth-century acts and charters gave the Colony a separate-but-equal status under the Crown. Unfortunately these acts were not taken seriously

194

in Great Britain; by the middle of the eighteenth century, the centralizing trend that was taking place had no respect for ancient charters. Richard Lee's grandfather sat on the Royal Executive Council at Williamsburg, which was the Virginia upper house, and his father received the same honor.

His father, Thomas Lee, had a rare vision early in the century. He told friends that he foresaw that America would someday become a great nation in its own right, and that the *capital of the independent sovereignties would be established near the little falls of the Potomac.* This region of Virginia at the time was sparsely settled frontier, remote from the tidewater tobacco plantations. The scenery was attractive, but the soil was poor, and few colonials sought lands along the Potomac. An unlikely spot, then, for such a capital.

Thomas Lee, however, purchased several tracts of land near these little falls, although these were distant from the older Lee properties. Thus Lee holdings' were within three miles of the spot where the United States capitol actually was erected; and on original Lee property, some of the most hallowed spots of the new nation, including Arlington Cemetery, would be established.

Thomas Lee's son Richard Henry was born at "Stratford," in Westmoreland County, in 1732. As a young patrician, descended from King's Councillors on both sides, he was privately tutored, then sent to England for schooling at Wakefield in Yorkshire. He returned to Virginia in 1752, in time to assume command of a company called the Westmoreland Volunteers in the French and Indian War. He offered the services of this company to General Edward Braddock as that officer passed through on his way to Fort Duquesne. Perhaps fortunately for the American nation, Braddock spurned the use of *provincial troops*, and Richard Henry Lee did not march to disaster in Pennsylvania. Young Lee's interest in the west was genuine: his father was one of the founders of the Ohio Company.

Richard Henry followed his ancestors' habit of public service. He became a justice of the peace in 1757, and the next year stood for Burgesses, as the Virginia assembly was called. In Virginia, while these seats were reserved to the gentry by use and wont, they were greatly vied for by the eligible families. Men like Lee sat in the legislature at Williamsburg usually at considerable personal expense. In the same year he began his public career he married Anne Aylett, of "Chantilly."

During his early years in Burgesses, Lee showed a deference to both the royal authority and older men. But young Lee was a brilliant example, almost the archetype, of the progressive, inherently liberal Virginia aristocrat. He was not so much democratic in spirit, as the word came to be used in America, but libertarian. He had no feeling that men were, or should be, equal, but he developed a deep distrust of human government and arbitrary authority over the citizenry, gentry and yeomen alike. His only speech of merit during his freshman term in Burgesses was in defense of a bill to prohibit the further importation of slaves from Africa. Lee, with Thomas Jefferson, Edward Rutledge, and a considerable number of the Southern landed élite, although their fortunes were built on Negro bondage, looked upon human slavery as insupportable either by reason or English law—as a form of social gangrene. Lee proposed *to lay so heavy a duty on the importation of slaves, as effectually to put an end to that iniquituous and disgraceful traffic within the colony of Virginia.* In his opening statement, he warned that the consequences of his debate *will greatly affect posterity, as well as ourselves.* He could hardly guess, however, how greatly it would affect the fortunes of his state, and those of another Lee, who was also born at Stratford Hall and was to free his own slaves a hundred years later.

But the views of the more liberal gentry were not dominant. They could not be, because slaves were widely held; there was an enormous economic investment in them; and they were considered vital to the agriculture of the South. Of the half-million Negroes in America—20 per cent of the population—only a handful were owned by the old families of enlightened feelings and education. In spite of Lee's eloquence, his bill died a natural death in committee.

But this was only Richard Henry Lee's opening salvo. He was soon inquiring into the conduct of the Royal Treasurer of Virginia and was thrown into alliance with Patrick

Henry on this matter and the "two-penny act." These activities, and his stand on slavery, made Lee prominent and popular among western Virginians, who had much of the same sentiments as western Carolinians and Pennsylvanians. These views naturally deeply offended the high Royalist faction in the colony, as any calling of government into question was bound to do.

Lee was immediately opposed to the British Parliamentary tax measures of 1763–1764. In March, 1764, he declared that *free possession of property, the right to be governed by laws made by our own representatives, and the illegality of taxation without consent* were *essential liberties of the British Constitution.* Just because they lived in America, colonials had *forefeited none of the blessings of that free government of which they were members.* The source of Lee's views is reasonably certain: his notebook indicates that John Locke and Charles Louis de Montesquieu were his favorite writers.

In May, 1764, he prophesied to an English correspondent that the acts of Parliament, designed to incorporate America more tightly within the British realm, could lead to independence instead. Again in 1764, Lee drafted a protest against the proposed Stamp Act which Burgesses passed and sent on to the King and House of Lords. Royal Governor Francis Fauquier, declared Lee's wording was *warm and indecent.*

The passage of the Stamp Act in 1765 threw Lee entirely into resistance to the royal party, and into a close relationship with Patrick Henry. He became head of what was called *a mob of gentlemen*—the Virginia Sons of Liberty. He formed the Westmoreland Association to boycott British goods. These measures in Virginia, which were also occurring in all the colonies, made the Stamp Act unenforce-able. Lee argued that, if Parliament *may take from me one shilling in the pound . . . what security have I for the other nineteen,* thus raising and impressing upon the Virginia public the fearful concept of the opening wedge of taxes that would continually increase but never be remitted. Lee's "Westmoreland Resolutions" against the Stamp Act were signed by more than one hundred prominent citizens, in-cluding virtually every great family in the section. George Washington signed, and was heard to say that Parliament had no more right to put its hand in his pocket than he in theirs.

Two years later, Lee described the Townshend Acts as *arbitrary, unjust, and destructive.* He said on the floor of Burgesses that the suspension of the New York Assembly, where Philip Livingston was leading similar resistance, *hangs like a flaming sword over our heads.* He urged the formation of Committees of Correspondence in 1768, but Virginia only began these in 1773.

During these years, Lee and Henry emerged as the two great leaders of the Whigs. Lee had more influence with the important gentry, and he is generally given credit for building the increasing resentment toward the royal au-thority among the upper class. He was also building a tre-mendous reputation for oratory. Practice gave him polish. He was nicknamed "Cicero," and once Edmund Pendleton accused him of practicing his gestures before a mirror. However he came by them, his movements and words on the floor made one member of Burgesses, St. George Tucker, feel Lee was *some being inspired with more than mortal powers of embellishment.* Lee believed a violent attempt was being made to destroy the inherent rights and liberties of British America; more important, his skill and leadership were drawing the power structure of Virginia along with him.

These years of Whig leadership were not personally profitable to him. Lee had rented out his rather modest inherited lands so he would be free for public affairs, and his private affairs did not prosper. He lived simply at Chantilly, the Aylett home, which was an unimpressive frame house, with a magnificent view of the Potomac. Anne Aylett Lee died in 1768, leaving him with four small children, and his own health was not good. He remarried, and tried his hand as a tobacco merchant, but he was never very successful in business.

Lee and Patrick Henry were joined in the legislature by a new liberal light, Thomas Jefferson. These men, though very different personally, were all completely united on the principles of American liberty. Jefferson and Lee together *cooked up* (a favorite Lee expression) the Burgesses' resolution *to celebrate the closing of Boston with fasting, humiliation, and prayer.* Here an important test was passed— the Crown had failed to divide and conquer. Virginia and Massachusetts did not trade with each other; they were very different colonies, with different economies and conditions, but they were united in the spirit of older English liberties and both aware of common danger. Other colonies supported Massachusetts in spirit, but, in Virginia, men like Lee and Jefferson made it very clear that the colonies were to stand together. Both provinces formed Committees of Correspondence at the same time, *to watch the conduct of the British Parliament, to spread more widely correct information on topics connected with the interests of the colonies, and to form a closer union of the men of influence in each.* Such activities had been carried on privately for five years; in 1773 they became official, with the sanction of the legislatures.

The reaction of Virginia, especially, to the Intolerable Acts, directed primarily against Massachusetts Bay, seems to have taken the British Ministry by surprise. Correspondence had made the concept of no taxation without representation universal in America, and spread the sentiment that an attack on one was an offense against all. A *closer union*, closer than anyone perhaps realized at the time, had been formed.

The passage by Burgesses of the Lee-Jefferson resolution of support for Boston caused the governor to dissolve the House, as rebellious and unruly. However, an Indian war—Lord Dunmore's War—broke out on the western frontier, and Governor Lord Dunmore found it necessary to recall the legislature in order to raise funds and troops for defense. The House of Burgesses did this quickly. Then, in August, 1774, it took action closer to its heart and mind. Three members, Lee, Henry, and George Washington, were dispatched to the Continental Congress at Philadelphia which the Committees of Correspondence had called.

At Philadelphia, Richard Henry Lee did most of the talking for Virginia, although the delegation eventually included some extremely capable men: Peyton Randolph (elected President), Benjamin Harrison, Edmund Pendleton, and Richard Bland, as well as Washington and Henry. At forty-two, Lee was slim and red-haired, with almost no trace of grey; he had brilliant, dominating eyes, and he carried his left hand, which he had injured, in a black silk handerchief. One of the best, if not the best, speakers in America, Lee caught all eyes.

Washington was still moderate and deliberately reserved,

and Henry, although he said in his opening address, *The distinctions between Virginians, Pennsylvanians, New Yorkers, and New Englanders, are no more. I am not a Virginian, but an American,* was too identified with radicalism and popular democracy to make a good impression on this generally conservative body. Lee was the bearer of a famous name, a man of deep conservative instincts, but fired by liberal principles. The combination, in a man of his talents, was irresistible.

Lee and John Adams found themselves very close in the First Congress. They were more advanced than the majority. With Roger Sherman of Connecticut, Patrick Henry, and Christopher Gadsden of South Carolina, the Adamses and Lee formed the nucleus of the "violent" party. Lee was for strong action, although he personally believed, all through the First Congress, that petitions would bring redress. His own draft to the King, however, was considered too inflammatory; the eventual conciliatory document was redrawn by John Dickinson.

He did not have the entire support of, but rather considerable opposition from, his own delegation. Harrison and Pendleton were much more cautious and conservative. John Adams remarked on this, adding that he and Samuel Adams were *very intimate with Mr. Lee . . . but Harrison, Pendleton, and others showed their jealousy. . . .*

In the Second Congress Lee was joined by three men more amenable to the idea of independence, which he had already decided upon. These were his brother Francis Lightfoot Lee, Thomas Jefferson, and George Wythe. Lee continued the work of carrying forward the "violent" position; in March, 1776, he and Wythe joined in proclaiming that George III, not the Ministry, was the author of American miseries. This was not historically valid, though it was the dominant view of the Congress. It was particularly important, since the hope of the moderates was to petition the King over the head of Parliament, and the great stumbling block to declaring independence was the symbol of the Crown. But if the Crown itself had turned against the colonists, then there could be no other redress—and this argument was clearly, if mistakenly, detailed in the final Declaration.

Lee was extremely influential, if not instrumental, in getting Virginia to instruct for independence in May, 1776. In a letter to Burgesses from Philadelphia, he wrote: *We are heavily clogged with instructions from these shameful Proprietary people and this will continue till Virginia sets the example of taking up government and sending peremptory orders to their delegates to pursue the most effectual measures of the Security of America*—specifically, independence. Burgesses then passed such a resolution. Acting on these orders, Lee proposed his dramatic motion to Congress on June 7.

Virginia was the richest and most populous of the American colonies, and the effect of its taking the lead carried great and historic weight.

Lee's most effective speeches in Congress were in support of his motion:

Why still deliberate? Let this happy day give birth to an American republic. Let her arise not to devastate and to conquer, but to reestablish the reign of peace and law. The eyes of Europe are fixed on us; she demands of us a living example of freedom, that may exhibit a contrast . . . to the ever increasing tyranny which desolates her polluted shores. She invites us to prepare an asylum, where the unhappy

*may find solace, and the persecuted repose. . . . if we are
not this day wanting in our duty, the names of the American legislators of 1776 will be placed by posterity, at the
side of Theseus, Lycurgus, and Romulus, of the three
Williams of Nassau, and of all those whose memory has
been, and ever will be, dear to virtuous men and good
citizens.*

It was customary that the mover of a carrying proposition be granted the honor of the chair of the committee
bringing it into execution. Richard Henry Lee, nevertheless, was not appointed to the committee that prepared
the Declaration. Thomas Jefferson, who was admittedly a
superior writer, if not so great a speaker, was given the
task of drafting the Declaration, while Lee himself returned to Virginia. It was commonly supposed by contemporary historians that Lee's withdrawal was due to his
wife's illness at home. Anne Pinckard Lee was sick, but
John Adams' own admission must be closer to the truth:
Lee had too many enemies in Congress, including a few of
the Virginia delegation. At that, Jefferson had to be chosen
over opposition from the moderates, who wanted the lukewarm Benjamin Harrison to do the writing.

This must have been a disappointment to Richard Henry
Lee, but at any rate the ideas of the Virginians, who gave
so much to the ideals of America, had already flowed together and blended. Either Jefferson or Lee could have
written the document and it would have emerged easily
recognizable, since the ideas Jefferson incorporated in it
seem to have had a common source. Jefferson, author of the
Summary View of the Rights of British America, which
had an explosive effect on educated Americans and set the
stage for the more widespread currency of *Common Sense,*

like Lee, drew many of his concepts from fellow Virginian George Wythe.

George Wythe

Wythe (it rhymed with Smith) was born in Back River, Virginia, to an old family which had been established since about 1680. Wythe, however, was a younger son, and, under the Virginia law of primogeniture, his older brother inherited the family estate. His mother was an unusually cultivated woman. Unable to educate George fashionably—primogeniture disinherited widows, too—she taught him Latin and Greek herself. He was able to attend the College of William and Mary only briefly, then secured a place reading law with Stephen Dewey of Prince George County. He was admitted to the Virginia bar in 1746, when he was twenty.

Wythe married, but his bride died. He practiced law indifferently for some years; he gave himself up to sorrow and dissipation. At the age of thirty he had accomplished nothing. Then, the death of his older brother made as dramatic a turn in his fortunes as the tragic death of Lawrence Washington worked on his young half-brother George. Like Washington, George Wythe came into the large family estate in 1755. He reformed, married Elizabeth Taliaferro of "Powhatan" and moved to Williamsburg. He plunged into work. He had always possessed a keen mind, and now he embarked on a brilliant career that was to span fifty years.

Wythe is more remembered for his friends, and his

effect on them, than what he did or said himself. When Francis Fauquier became royal governor of Virginia in 1758, Wythe was one of his closest colonial friends; both men were extremely cultivated and erudite. Even more important, Wythe took a young man named Thomas Jefferson into his law office, became his mentor, and sponsored him at the bar. Jefferson's remonstrances against Parliament came from Wythe more than from Richard Henry Lee.

In 1764 Wythe held that England and Virginia were coördinate nations, united only by common sovereignty under the Crown. This was six years before James Wilson published a similar statement; Wythe is generally recognized as the originator of the concept that eventually became the cement of the British Commonwealth of Nations.

This concept was a great force toward independence, once it became evident that George III would not, or could not, recognize the principle. When Wythe, with Lee, sounded the proclamation that the King was the author of colonial *miseries,* a long span in the bridge to independence was hammered in place. If George III "abdicated" his responsibilities toward his separate but equal subjects across the sea in favor of Parliament, which had no jurisdiction in American eyes, then there was no recourse but official independence.

Besides formulating many of Jefferson's ideas, Wythe was a member of Burgesses who regularly lined up behind Richard Henry Lee. One remonstrance he drew up was thought so bold—almost treasonous—that Burgesses modified it. As a strong Whig, Wythe came to the Second Continental Congress in September, 1775, joining his former student. In Congress, he became *one of our best men* to Adams. He was one of the first to advocate seeking foreign alliances, some months before July, 1776. He seconded Lee in the independence debate in June.

Rush called him A *profound lawyer. . . . I have seldom known a man possess more modesty, or a more dovelike simplicity and gentleness of manner. . . .* Because he was modest, his effectiveness was regularly behind the scenes, rather than on the floor. With Thomas Jefferson and George Mason, he was one of the three men who were most influential in the establishment of Virginia's new government in 1776–1777. He also designed the state seal.

Lee himself held no bitterness toward Jefferson for assuming what he must have considered his own task of honor. Jefferson sent both him and Wythe copies of the original draft, and the document adopted after revision. Lee commiserated with Jefferson on the anti-slavery parts' deletion in deference to consensus politics, but added, *The Thing in its nature is so good, that no Cookery can spoil the Dish for the palates of Freemen.*

The part Richard Henry Lee took in advocating independence was well known to the British. It made him a particular target for reprisal. The British government was determined that two men—George Washington and he— would have to be surrendered as a preliminary to negotiations, had British arms prevailed in 1776. A little-known fact was that Lee had two sons at a public school in England when he supported Revolution. These boys were taunted and badgered by classmates *in the garb and rank of gentlemen* who hoped *their father's head might soon be seen set on a pike on Tower Hill.* The sons were not harmed, although they stoutly defended their sire.

Lee's brother William had emigrated to England, where he became High Sheriff of London, the only American ever to hold this office. This Lee was a loyal British subject, but he opposed the war policy of the Ministry and Parliament throughout the Revolutionary War. Before the break, he supplied his brothers in America with much vital information as to the intents of Parliament; his letters undoubtedly had much to do with Richard Henry's belief that reconciliation had become impossible. On September 10, 1774, William Lee wrote: *From these Acts [the Intolerable Acts] it is evident that open war is intended against you. . . . you have no alternative but to resist united and most probably be free, or to submit and be slaves at once. . . . these pimps and parasites, the present Ministry, being instigated by the Devil and led on by their wicked and corrupt hearts. . . .* Needless to say, William Lee was an English Whig.

Despite the fact that the Lee family had powerful friends in London, Richard Henry was not spared persecution. Just after Lee had returned from Congress in June, 1776, a British warship landed a strong party of Royal Marines in Westmoreland County. This force marched up to Lee's house on the Potomac and broke down the door at midnight. Fortunately, Lee, who was in the county, was visiting a friend some miles away. A British captain bullied the terrified house slaves, and even offered them a gold guinea in return for revealing their master's location. The Negroes all swore Lee was still in Pennsylvania. Frustrated, the Marines went away.

Lee's services on the more important Congressional committees are well known. His war services in Virginia are not. He was appointed Lieutenant of Westmoreland, in which post he commanded the local militia, with the rank of colonel. Lee kept the local forces at full strength, fully armed and equipped. His preparations were so effective that Nathanael Greene wrote that the British, who sent frequent raiding parties ashore along the Potomac, *could not set foot in Westmoreland without having the militia immediately set upon them.* They avoided the area scrupulously, though other counties suffered.

Colonel Lee himself fought on one occasion. Seeing a British tender put into a cove inside his territory, Lee, on horseback, led a charge of foot soldiers to capture it, galloping into the shallow river water. The long guns from the British men-of-war in the Potomac opened up. Lee's horse was shot from under him, and his men driven to cover. Although he was left on foot only a few yards from a boatful of enemy sailors, Lee got to his feet and, rallying his men, retreated in good order under heavy fire.

From 1780 through 1782 he declined further elections to Congress, preferring to work in the House of Burgesses. Virginia was painfully erecting new principles of government and setting precedents for all America, and Lee was deeply engaged in these questions: payment of debts and paper money, disestablishment of the Church and taxation to support the clergy. He was generally considered to have turned "conservative" after 1780.

But Lee was not inconsistent; he was and always had been a patrician libertarian—not a social democrat. He fought against cheap paper money, although the poorer classes wanted it. He was uneasy at the secularization of the state. He was particularly adamant against the repudiation of British debts, as a breach of individual and national honor. When a popular bill was proposed to wipe out all private debt to British merchants and others as a war measure, Lee battled this strenuously, saying: *It would have been better to remain the honest slaves of Britain than to become dishonest freemen.* His motives were pure, but that, as with his opposition to slavery, did not make him popular, either with poor farmers or planters. He was more often than not on the losing side.

He had spent his life battling British authority and he was reluctant to surrender hard-won liberties to an American substitute. Like Jefferson, he had a basic distrust of all human government. He feared to give the Congress *power of both purse and sword*. One speech summed up the aristocratic Virginian ideal of freedom magnificently:

The first maxim of a man who loves liberty should be never to grant Rulers an atom of power that is not most clearly and indispensably necessary for the Safety and well-being of Society.

He was far-seeing. He was one of those who insisted that the treaty of peace include America's expansion to the Mississippi, and he also supported Virginia's cession of its territorial claims to the Northwest. In 1784, the Congress, meeting in New York, broke rotation among the states and chose him President of the Congress—the highest position of honor in America—out of an almost unanimous sentiment that he was the most worthy member in its ranks. In 1787, Lee was responsible for the veto on slavery north of the Ohio in the Northwest Ordinance.

He helped write sound money principles into the Constitution, but he opposed the Constitution because the finished version lacked guarantees of personal freedoms. When Virginia ratified it, he took on one last task in search of liberty. Elected his state's first senator in 1789, he went to Congress and was instrumental in seeing that the Virginian brand of liberalism was written forever into the national document, in the form of the first ten amendments to the Constitution, the Bill of Rights.

His work was finished. His failing health broke completely, and Richard Henry Lee died in modest circumstances at home in 1794. On the Potomac, Chantilly crumbled and disappeared in ruins, but it is not too much to say that Lee's spirit eventually reached from sea to sea.

Francis Lightfoot Lee

Francis Lightfoot Lee, a younger brother of Richard Henry, the "Stratford" line, *having more men of merit in it than any other family,* was born too late to attend school in England like his brothers. He lived the quiet life of a country gentleman in Loudon. He was a Lee, although an overshadowed one; he went to Burgesses, and in 1776 to Congress. There he signed the Declaration, risking his all, but as soon afterward as he gracefully could, he retired to private life.

Benj Harrison

The Virginia delegations to the several Congresses were studded with famous names. George Washington and Peyton Randolph were two of the foremost landowners in America. One died as President of Congress, before the

Declaration; the other gained everlasting fame with his ragged Continentals. Another scion of a great American family who signed the Declaration was Benjamin Harrison.

The first Harrison settled in Surrey, or "Surry," Virginia, around 1640. His son, born in 1645, had the honorific "Honourable" inscribed on his tombstone; his sons were prominent squires. The Harrison clan prospered in Virginia; they married Carters and Randolphs and erected a magnificent seat on the James River near Petersburg, where Benjamin Harrison was born about 1726.

He attended the College of William and Mary, but did not graduate, supposedly due to a quarrel with a professor. The county sent him to Burgesses before he was twenty-one. He lacked the legal age to sit, but he was a Harrison, of a family noted for its sense of public duty and strong common sense, so the members overlooked his single fault. In Burgesses Harrison could not help but be an influential man; he had blood or marriage ties to virtually every powerful family in the Colony, and in eighteenth-century America this was more important than it is now.

The Royal Governor cultivated him, and elevated him to the Royal Executive Council, the colony's provincial "House of Lords." In spite of this Harrison became a great disappointment to the royalist faction; he was a member of the committee that supported the Stamp Act protest of 1764. He came firmly into Richard Henry Lee's camp as a Whig. He was a logical choice for the First Congress in 1774.

John Adams was impressed with him on first meeting. *These gentlemen of Virginia appear to be the most spirited and consistent of any. Harrison said he would have come on foot rather than not come.*

Harrison, however, lagged considerably behind Lee and Patrick Henry in revolutionary spirit. In March, 1775, he opposed Henry's motion in Burgesses to place Virginia into a *posture of defence.* Outvoted, he agreed to serve on the committee that did so. In May, 1775, he was returned to Congress, where he roomed with Washington and Randolph. A heavy, hearty, jovial man, Harrison appears to have been popular with most delegates. After Peyton Randolph returned to Virginia, Harrison was one who supported John Hancock for the Presidency of Congress. According to one story, when Hancock demurred, Harrison seized the elegant Bostonian and lifted him into the presiding chair. *We'll show mother Britain how little we care for her,* he boomed, *by making a Massachusetts man our president, whom she has excluded from pardon by public proclamation!*

This move irritated John Adams, who was no "favorite" of Hancock's. Harrison was of the "cold party" toward independence also, however spirited he had seemed before. All of this led Adams, whose acuteness was often modified by what can only be called political prejudice, to write *This [Harrison] was an indolent, luxurious, heavy gentleman, of no use in Congress or committee, but a great embarrassment to both.*

This is not an accepted view. Benjamin Harrison did important work on three vital committees: state, war, and navy. He was made chairman of the Committee of the Whole, from which chair he presided over the final debates on independence. Rush's description gives another clue as to Adams' animosity: *He had strong State prejudices, and was very hostile to the leading characters from . . . New England. . . . He was upon the whole a useful member of Congress 'and sincerely devoted to the welfare of his country.*

Harrison like Rutledge and some others from both North and South, suspected the New Englanders of "leveling tendencies"; Adams, although he was no democrat, apparently gave many of the more aristocratic gentry in Congress this impression. Some of these hostilities, more suspected than real, impeded the affairs of Congress. Adams and Harrison treated each other politely, while Adams and Lee were *intimate*. This in turn led to coolness between Harrison and Lee.

Adams was again disappointed when Hancock appointed Harrison Chairman of the Whole or presiding officer of the Whole Congress when engaged in important debate. He wanted Governor Samuel Ward of Rhode Island in that chair; Ward was a staunch "violent." At any rate, Ward shortly afterward contracted smallpox and died. Despite Adams' fears that Harrison was a tool of the moderates, his work in the chair was praised by all as *decisive and fair*.

Although Harrison signed the Declaration, he was not returned to Congress, in a general clearance of the "cold" or moderate men. He was active at home and served as a state councillor. He was returned to Congress briefly, but most of his service was in the state. He sat in Burgesses until 1781, and afterward was three times governor. He died as a United States Representative in 1791.

Benjamin Harrison lost heavily in the war. His shipyard on the James River was burned and destroyed; many cargoes he shipped as his own merchant were lost to British action. But the family went on to even greater distinction: the third son of Benjamin Harrison became the ninth President of the United States, and a great-grandson, also named Benjamin, its twenty-third.

Carter Braxton.

The most reluctant of all the Virginia rebels was Carter Braxton, who was sent to Philadelphia in January, 1776, to replace Peyton Randolph, who had died. Braxton was suspected of British prejudices. Joseph Reed of Pennsylvania wrote George Washington in March, *It is said the Virginians are so alarmed with the Idea of Independence that they have sent Mr. Braxton on Purpose to turn the Vote of that Colony, if any Question on that Subject should come before Congress.* Certainly, his appointment was secured by the moderate faction in Burgesses, those Virginians who were still desperately trusting to a hope of reconciliation.

Carter Braxton was born to velvet and silver buckles; his mother, like Benjamin Harrison's, was a daughter of "King" Robert Carter, President of the Royal Executive Council, and the most powerful colonial in Virginia. Braxton inherited rich lands, attended the College of William and Mary, and married a young lady of fine estate. This girl died in childbirth, leaving Braxton, at twenty-one, with an infant daughter. He went to England that same year, 1757, and did not return until 1760. On his return he married Elizabeth Corbin, daughter of the King's Receiver-General of the Customs. From this marriage there were sixteen children, ten of whom survived.

Braxton moved to King William County from King and Queen; he had estates in both counties. He was very rich: he held broad lands growing tobacco and Indian corn, many slaves, and large sums in colonial currency. He erected a fine house called Elsing Green on the Pawmunkey, or Pamunkey, and, later, a great seat "Chericoke." He lived as a grand squire and, in 1761, he entered Burgesses.

In politics, he was always described as more conservative than the run of planters. He did sign Lee's *Resolutions* in 1769, agreeing that only Burgesses had the right to tax Virginians. But Braxton abhorred two things: popular democracy and separation from the empire. He was a man caught in between, and his great—though failing—work, was to effect a compromise.

He had so much faith that a compromise would be found that, in early 1775, he placed most of his capital in a fleet of ships sailing under the Union Jack. To subsidize this mercantile venture, he mortgaged his estates heavily. At the very time he executed this decision, the Ministry sent orders to American governors to seize the public armories, and the export of munitions to the colonies was prohibited. Britain was moving toward a war footing.

The attempt to execute this order precipitated the Massachusetts storm. There might well have been similar bloodshed in Virginia for the same reason—except for Carter Braxton. Governor Lord Dunmore ordered the public magazines withdrawn and stored aboard British warships on April 20, 1775. This news provoked a near-riot. Word flashed from the taverns of Williamsburg into the country. The reaction was quite similar to the reaction in Massachusetts when the redcoats marched toward Lexington. Peyton Randolph, who was in Williamsburg, tried to soothe tempers, but the militia assembled under arms.

Patrick Henry, who was spoiling for a showdown, came marching into Williamsburg at the head of a contingent of Hanover volunteers. The sight of armed men provoked Lord Dunmore into debarking some Marines from H.M.S.

Fowey to stand guard around his palace. Just when a collision seemed inevitable, Carter Braxton worked out a shaky compromise, through his father-in-law, Colonel Corbin. The governor was permitted to retain the munitions, but only upon the agreement to pay into the colonial treasury their full value. Corbin made out a bill of reimbursement, drawn on Philadelphia.

Bloodshed was narrowly averted, but the situation was too volatile and tempers too high for it to remain quiet. Dunmore, when he realized a few scarlet coats and a Marine guard would not deter Burgesses, abandoned the palace and took refuge on the *Fowey.* Thus on June 7, 1775, the royal government ended.

Carter Braxton, the man in between, served on the Committee of Safety, but he still worked for compromise. The ground was cut from under him over the ensuing months, and reluctantly, but bravely, he signed the Declaration in 1776.

With Harrison he was dropped from the Congress in 1776, but he was elected to the House of Representatives under the new state constitution.

Th⁵ Nelson jr.

Another Virginian who lived in the style of Braxton and Harrison was Thomas Nelson, Jr., of York. His grandfather was founder of the town, and built the first customs house in the colony. His father had extended the family fortune through shipping tobacco and buying broad estates. William Nelson served as President of the Executive

Council, like "King" Carter, and for a time was acting royal governor and presiding judge of the colonial supreme court. His grand style of living was proverbial in York. On one occasion he bought Lord Baltimore's six white coach horses, just to give his own black animals a rest.

William Nelson sent his son Thomas Junior (the "Junior" was meant to indicate he was the eldest of five sons, an important point under the law of primogeniture) to Hackney, followed by Trinity College at Cambridge. One of Nelson's tutors was Dr. Beilby Porteous, who later became Bishop of London. Many years afterward, Thomas Nelson told Benjamin Rush that of nine or ten Virginians educated with him at this time in England, all but he became Tories.

In 1762 Nelson married Lucy Grymes, daughter of Colonel Philip Grymes of Middlesex. William Nelson provided a large house for the young couple, who embarked upon a grand social round. There were a dozen *genteel and opulent families* in the vicinity of York, or Yorktown as it came to be called, and these people formed a brilliant social circle, entertaining widely and expensively among themselves. In a Virginia famed for this kind of hospitality, Thomas Nelson, Jr., soon became noted for his own lavish generosity. He could afford it; his father left him a large plantation, plus about £30,000 sterling in notes on call at London.

Nelson had been impressed with the life of English country gentry during his sojourn in the old country. Back home, he dressed and acted the part of the wealthy landed squire. In good weather, he rode out to his fields, accompanied by a Negro gunbearer, who carried his fowling piece. He maintained a fine pack of hounds, and during the winter season he rode in fox hunts with his York circle once or twice a week.

It was an idyllic existence for the man Rush described as a *respectable country gentleman*. It was written in Virginia that *no Gent. ever stopped an hour in York, without receiving an invitation to Mr. Nelson's hospitality.*

Nelson does not seem to have been involved in resistance prior to 1774, the year he was elected to Burgesses from York. This was the assembly dissolved by Lord Dunmore for passing strongly worded resolutions against the Boston Port Bill at the instigation of Lee and Jefferson. This outraged Tom Nelson as much as Whigs of long standing; he was one of 89 members who met extra-legally the next day at a tavern in Williamsburg and recommended that Virginia send deputies to a general, or Continental, Congress to discuss American grievances. He was returned to the next Burgesses and participated in sending seven delegates to Philadelphia.

A bluff, honest, not particularly intellectual squire, Nelson found himself hotly supporting Patrick Henry's resolution to put the colony in a posture of defense in March, 1775. Nelson agreed with Henry's words about liberty or death, which were then too radical for a majority of the older gentry. He argued for a *well-regulated militia, composed of gentlemen and yeomen.*

In the munitions-seizure crisis of April, 1775, Nelson nevertheless tried to protect Lord Dunmore from Henry's Hanover troops, because he believed the governor would give satisfaction. However, British sailors debarked from a warship near York and threatened Nelson's uncle, who served as secretary to the executive council. The captain of H.M.S. *Fowey* sent a letter stating Yorktown would be bombarded if harm came to Lord Dunmore. This sat poorly with honest Tom Nelson.

He shouted from the floor of Burgesses: *I am a merchant of Yorktown, but I am a Virginian first. Let my trade perish. I call God to witness that if any British troops are landed in the County of York, of which I am Lieutenant, I will wait no orders, but will summon the militia and drive the invaders into the sea!* Nelson's property and family remained in Yorktown, which was exposed to the sea and the Royal Navy on three sides. Friends feared for their safety, and also knew that Nelson had vast sums tied up in notes in Great Britain. They warned him to desist; he was jeopardizing himself and his fortune beyond the call of duty. The British flag still waved over the House of Burgesses this spring, and Nelson's talk was as inflammatory as Henry's.

But this show of independence caused Nelson to be elected Colonel of the Second Virginia Regiment in July. Henry was elected to command the First. And in August, 1775, Nelson was sent with George Wythe to the Congress at Philadelphia. Here Adams noted that he was a *fat man, a speaker, and alert and lively for his weight.*

The rejection of the Olive Branch Petition and the news that the King was recruiting German mercenaries—*all the powers of Hell are to be let loose on us*, Rutledge wrote—disgusted Nelson with the moderates, or cold party. He opted for independence as early as February, 1776. In a letter to John Page, from whom he wanted to get the feelings of his constituents, he wrote that it was impossible to *have any affection for a people who are carrying on the most savage war against us.* He also mentioned he feared a majority of the Congress were like a *weak, enervated*

*woman. . . . Would you think that we have some among
us, who still expect honorable proposals from the [Brit-
ish] Administration?*

Nelson was in Williamsburg in May, 1776, when the
Colony of Virginia dissolved its old Burgesses in favor of a
general convention, which immediately assumed authority
and government. This was the de facto Virginia revolution.
On May 14, Nelson, through coördination with Henry, had
the honor of placing before the convention a resolution of
independence—the motion Richard Henry Lee had requested from Philadelphia. Edmund Randolph, in writing
about this choice, and Nelson's subsequent *rough oratory*,
mentioned that Nelson's chief characteristic was that he
had no fears *of his own*, and could hardly understand
anyone else's. The public was already in favor of independence, and when Henry added his own oratory standing
as a pillar of fire, the motion carried. Revolution was de
jure, and official.

Nelson galloped off for Congress, to lay the resolution,
and new orders for the Virginia delegation, before Richard
Henry Lee. Both Lee and General Washington, who was
in the city, were delighted with the news.

Nelson left Congress in May, 1777, apparently due to illness. But he continued in the Virginia legislature, and also
as Lieutenant of York County. The Lieutenant was the
chief magistrate, civil and military, of each Virginia county.
It was a post of great responsibility and honor, originally
filled by the royal governor's appointee. The Lieutenant
presided over all courts of justice, and as chief of militia
carried the title of colonel. The office was unpaid, but
sought after by prominent families. Every former Lieutenant bore his military title for life, and this custom pro-

voked some amusement, in other parts of the country, with the proliferation of Southern colonels. The custom was so deep-seated that it was carried on after independence, though the civil responsibilities were divorced from the office.

Like Colonel Lee of Westmoreland County, Colonel Nelson was an energetic militia chief. He handled his post so well and generated so much confidence—though he was not a military type, or a soldier of genius—that in August, 1777, he was appointed commander-in-chief of Virginia forces, with the rank of brigadier, in the Howe invasion scare. For a time it was feared General Howe's armada would descend on the Virginia coast, but Howe sailed up the Chesapeake and made for Philadelphia.

In the spring of 1778, Nelson raised a company of Virginia cavalry *to serve at their own expense* in Pennsylvania. He went to Philadelphia at the head of this contingent, acting not only as commander, but the company's banker, too. Most of the funds expended in this service came from his own pocket, for which he received the thanks of Congress in August, when General Sir Henry Clinton had evacuated Pennsylvania, and the Virginia troops were released.

Nelson was well chosen as Virginia's leading soldier. The war governors, Patrick Henry and Thomas Jefferson in turn, were not military men, and it is charitable to say they lacked even an elemental grasp of military matters. Here they differed sharply from George Washington, who knew well that no hasty standing to arms of a militia of *gentlemen and yeomen* farmers could keep the British in effective check, or win a decisive victory to end the war. Jefferson disliked the concept of a standing army; this was probably the only flaw in his vast genius. He saw a standing military force, even during the war, as a threat to liberty. There is no question but that Virginia, the richest and most populous state, shirked its military responsibilities in the Revolution. Under Henry and Jefferson it not only failed to support the Continentals adequately, but also starved its own local forces.

This threw a great personal burden on General Tom Nelson. He acted as military "banker" throughout the war. He lent money freely to any soldier or officer who was temporarily embarrassed. He put out thousands of pounds in this way, and one friend remarked that almost none of it ever came back. Nelson was not the kind of man to press a debt.

There was no provision for a regular force—which George Wythe argued for with Washington—but there were constant calls for war service from the small farmer militia due to British feints and raids. This worked tremendous hardship on the average farmer, who had no slaves or hired help, but had vital crops to harvest. To free some of the men in the County of York, Nelson neglected his own tobacco and sent his slaves and tenants to work in the fields of men called to service. He stripped his plantation of his fine hunting and carriage horses and gave them to the army. He fed the hungry militia of surrounding counties from his own granary. For all this, Nelson was acclaimed widely. *His credit stood high,* a Virginian wrote, *when the credit of the Commonwealth could not bring a sixpence into her treasury.* But Nelson was also being eaten out of house and home. On one occasion he personally paid the arrears of two regiments, one in York, and the other in Williamsburg.

In these same years that he took these losses like the gentleman he was, Nelson vehemently backed Richard Henry Lee's fight against the repudiation of British debts. Nelson angered many in the legislature by stating the question baldly and adding, *Whatever is voted, by God, I will pay my own debts like an honest man!*

In June, 1780, the State of Virginia was asked for $2,000,000 in specie to support the French fleet now operating in American waters. These allies could not be fed and supplied with paper Continental currency, because no farmer or merchant would accept it any longer. Nelson tried to help raise the money from wealthy Virginians, but he found himself unable to secure a copper on the state treasury's credit. He was told, *We won't lend the governor or government a shilling.*

The Virginia administration, like others, had issued too much paper in response to popular demand; further, a vast number of men who still had capital felt that a government which agreed to repudiate private British debts because of popular clamor, was not exactly trustworthy toward its own citizens. But Nelson was told, *We'll lend you, General Nelson, all the money we can raise.*

Nelson, like Robert Morris, agreed to put up his personal bond for the money. He pledged his tobacco, estates, and notes on call for it to various individuals. But unlike Morris, Nelson possessed no personal genius for making more money, or influence in Congress to get reimbursement. However, no man was more trusted by the public in 1780–1781, and when Thomas Jefferson's term of office expired in June, 1781, Nelson was elected governor. He took office at a time when Benedict Arnold and General William Phillips were raiding along the Virginia coast, and Lord Cornwallis' army had already moved within the state.

When General Horatio Gates was defeated at Camden, in South Carolina, in 1780, Washington detached Nathanael Greene to command the Southern Department, and this time there was no Congressional protest. Greene immediately took charge and began to fight a canny war of maneuver in the South. He divided his forces into two wings, one under himself and the other under tough old wagonmaster Daniel Morgan. These forces marched about, hitting here and there, continually confusing the British General Cornwallis, who wanted the Americans to stand and fight. But this was basically a guerrilla war, the only kind the less-heavily armed and poorly supplied Americans could win. Greene *danced* with the English Earl, as a contemporary popular ballad went, but to steps the British General could not seem to learn. Finally, on January 2, 1781, Cornwallis divided his own forces. He ordered Banastre Tarleton, who had risen from cornet of horse to a major commander since 1776, to find Daniel Morgan, fix him, and destroy him.

Tarleton took about 1,100 men and pursued Morgan. In one of the most brilliantly planned and executed battles in American history, the Virginian Dan Morgan allowed Tarleton to "trap" his force at Hannah's Cowpens, on the Broad River. Tarleton, over-eager, ordered his regulars to attack frontally, although they were tired from a five-hour march. Morgan, putting little trust in the green farmer militia, asked it to fire once and retire, while he kept his own disciplined Continentals in the center, in reserve.

The militia did better than Morgan had hoped. It fired a volley, retired, and then came back—on the British flank. Meanwhile, Tarleton's weary soldiers charged into an American buzzsaw. The Continental ranks held, and their deadly fire smashed the British waves. At the end,

Tarleton was able to flee the field with only 140 cavalry; leaving 90 per cent of his army killed, wounded, or captured.

Morgan, who had lost only twelve killed, immediately moved his army away from the Cowpens, avoiding Cornwallis, who was rushing up to close the "trap."

On March 18, 1781, Greene used a similar maneuver, baiting Cornwallis into attacking him frontally at Guilford Courthouse, in North Carolina. The British won the field, since Greene deliberately retreated in good order after giving the enemy a severe mauling. Washington's best field commander, Greene, in fact, was never to win a battle in the Revolutionary War. But at Guilford Courthouse Cornwallis lost a quarter of his men, and Greene, who lost many fewer, was still at large. Worse, he had moved into South Carolina behind Cornwallis' back, and was busily freeing the countryside from British rule. This was a classic guerrilla campaign. Everywhere Greene marched, the patriots rose; the Tories fled for protection to the British enclaves and forts.

Cornwallis, unable to cope with the situation, hastily retreated out of the threatening hinterland to the coast. He even abandoned 70 badly-wounded soldiers to American mercies. Cornwallis' overambitious decision to grasp the *ripe plum* of North Carolina had not only cost the British 3,000 men, but the British had marched 800 miles, fought several disastrous battles, and now were about to lose "safe" South Carolina. Greene confidently marched on Cornwallis' heels, riding the Carolinas of enemy influence. When Clinton heard this news at New York, he was almost apoplectic.

In fairness to Cornwallis, he, like Sir William Howe, was not an incompetent general by eighteenth-century European standards. The British commanders were fighting under conditions, and against a foe, they never quite understood. They were not marching across a land where the population was politically inert and, once regular forces were beaten, could easily be controlled. They were battling an entire people, the most difficult foe of all. The Tories were never effective. And the American ability to keep a small regular army—the Continentals—as an ever-dangerous nucleus of resistance made it impossible for the British to consolidate their military gains.

At this time the thought processes of Lord Cornwallis become very difficult to understand. Forced into a rest camp with the main British army at Wilmington, North Carolina, he made no attempt to rejoin Lord Rawdon at Camden, although Greene was now in South Carolina. Cornwallis knew that Rawdon lacked sufficient force to hold South Carolina against Greene. But he was frustrated and infuriated at his inability to fight the American general successfully. He devised a strategy of trying to carry the fight to the enemy, by rolling up the American rear. A *serious attempt upon Virginia would be the most solid plan*, he wrote. Ignoring two facts—that he had insufficient troops to capture Virginia, and that his orders still required him to hold South Carolina as a primary mission— he marched across the Virginia border with an army which, on May 20, 1781, comprised about 7,200 men.

Behind him, Greene, with the help of the local guerrillas, Andrew Pickens, Thomas Sumter, and Francis Marion, and "Light-Horse Harry" Lee (father of Robert E. Lee), attacked Rawdon's scattered posts one by one. Some surrendered, some held out with great gallantry. Rawdon fought energetically, but he was fighting the tide; even his victory at Hobkirk's Hill was Pyrrhic. By July 1, the

British were encircled in Charleston, and the British presence in the far south was limited to that city and Savannah. Rawdon, exhausted, gave up command and sailed for England, only to be captured by the French. Greene, content with freeing the countryside, took up a careful watch on the High Hills of the Santee.

Meanwhile, Cornwallis blundered into Virginia, and his rendezvous with Thomas Nelson, and destiny, at Yorktown.

The march of the British into Virginia hit the Signers hard. The manager of George Wythe's plantation defected to the enemy, turning over all Wythe's personal property and slaves. Wythe lost almost his entire fortune. This was a personal tragedy, but it became his country's gain, for it forced Wythe to continue in a chair of law at William and Mary. Here it is generally acknowledged that he *charted the way of American jurisprudence* at least through Henry Clay. In addition to his influence on Jefferson, there is reason to believe he gave James Wilson his concepts of judicial review. With Edmund Pendleton, he certainly was one of Virginia's two greatest legal minds. He was *magnificently ethical* in the manner of his time and class; he would not take a case he considered unjust. And significantly, he believed in representative, rather than, popular government. Two of his disciples, Jefferson and Madison, helped put it into effect, and another pupil, John Marshall, wrote his ideas on jurisprudence into United States precedents and law. Jefferson said he was a *model of future times* and began a biography that was never finished.

The destruction of his estate, which made him work on as America's first professor of law, thus had far-reaching effects. Wythe freed his few slaves before he died at eighty-one. Ironically, even at that advanced age, he was poisoned by a great-nephew who could not wait to inherit his remaining estate.

Th Jefferson

Having ruined Wythe, the British now tried to capture his most famous student, Jefferson. The former governor of Virginia had retired to his estate at Monticello on June 2, 1781. Tarleton, with his hand bandaged from wounds suffered in Carolina, trotted at the head of 250 horse to Charlottesville, hoping to seize the Virginia legislature meeting there. The assembly was forewarned and scattered. Tarleton now sent a flying troop on to Monticello.

A courier reached Jefferson in time. Jefferson put his family in a carriage and sent them to a neighbor's home for safety, but he himself remained behind until the red-coats were in sight. Persuaded that they were really after him, he fled and joined his family. The British party, deep in enemy territory, was too nervous to search him out. Nor did they pause to despoil or burn down Monticello, for which future generations can be thankful.

The next Signer to suffer was Carter Braxton, the reluctant rebel of the tidewater. Braxton had already lost the bulk of his fortune; when open warfare began his cargoes and ships were seized by the British at sea. He still had his estate and great house at Chericoke. But when the enemy invaders swept through, they burned it down, with all his furnishings and papers.

There was worse to come. Braxton had mortgaged his

lands to pay for the captured cargoes; when the notes came due, he could not pay. Certain assets he held in the form of notes were repaid in worthless currency. In the end, all Braxton's great properties were attached. He was not only ruined personally, but he dragged down two of his sons-in-law who had co-signed his notes. He died heartbroken in 1797. Only the generosity of numerous relatives saved his widow from absolute want.

The British army now marched toward the sea and Yorktown, where Thomas Nelson's warehouses, lands, and magnificent Georgian mansion stood.

Nelson, as governor of the state, took command of the Virginia militia. He put it under the command of Major General the Marquis de Lafayette, whom Washington sent south with part of the Continental Army. Cornwallis tried to corner Lafayette and bring him to battle. But the Americans had learned from their "old fox," General Washington. The young Frenchman, given high rank by Congress, refused to be sucked in. He had only 1,200 Continentals, and about the same number of Nelson's militia, against more than 7,000 British regulars. As he said wryly, *I am not yet strong enough to get beaten.* He "danced" with Cornwallis through the summer of 1781.

Unable to win a decisive vistory, and running low on supply, Cornwallis slowly backed into the York peninsula. Now, the British tragedy of errors became continent-wide. Sir Henry Clinton angrily dispatched orders Cornwallis ignored. The British fleet off America, worried now about the presence of a powerful French squadron under Admiral de Grasse, pursued its own interests and refused to worry about the army on land. When Cornwallis, expecting to be either resupplied or redeployed by sea by the Royal

Navy, stopped at Yorktown, he was suddenly in a potential trap.

It had never occurred to him or the British staff that Britannia might not always rule the waves. But now De Grasse appeared off the mouth of the Chesapeake; an American ally for the first time held naval supremacy along the Virginia coast. Washington, at New York, saw a sudden opportunity he might never have again. It was a chance to use his carefully hoarded regular Continentals in a final classic battle, to bring this classic guerrilla war to a close. He got the opportunity largely because Morris' money now enabled him to mount a campaign, and the specie Nelson signed for had kept a French fleet at sea.

Under carefully coördinated plans, Washington and General Comte de Rochambeau, with a strong French force, marched south from New York to Chesapeake Bay, where De Grasse ferried them across to Virginia. At the same time, Lafayette, under orders, moved from Richmond with a greatly strengthened force to fix Cornwallis on the York peninsula. Suddenly, in September, the largest single British army in North America was in a dangerous situation. The French fleet blockaded it by sea; its supplies were running out; and a superior force closed in by land.

By October 9, 1781, Washington's and Rochambeau's disciplined regulars had dug fortifications around Yorktown and were tightening their siege. A horde of Nelson's state troops stood in support. Washington had brought up heavy guns. A murderous fire from 70 cannon began to crash into the tiny town of York and destroy it piece by piece.

Thomas Nelson, Jr., was at the front with his men, although he was ill. Through his telescope, Nelson noticed that while American shot was demolishing British breast-works and the houses where British soldiers had taken cover, his own stately brick mansion stood untouched. The bodies of dead horses and grenadiers lay mangled all around, but his house miraculously escaped. Nelson knew the house was used as a British headquarters. His uncle, who had been allowed to pass out with other civilians, had reported the fact.

Nelson asked the gunners: *Why do you spare my house?*

An artilleryman replied, *Sir, out of respect to you.*

Give me the cannon! Nelson roared. At his insistence, a gun was leveled at the mansion; the first round sent a ball completely through it. British officers were killed inside, and the house was demolished.

For eight days this horrendous battering continued. The British ran out of fodder and had to kill their horses. The smallpox appeared among the tightly packed army. Cornwallis, hardly able to believe this was happening to him, seemed paralyzed. In New York, Clinton was equally lethargic, although a British general on his staff argued that continued inaction would doom Cornwallis and probably lose the war. A Loyalist at New York bitterly summed up Clinton's actions; he *had Parties of Girls in the Garden, in the Midst of . . . fears, and the Anxieties of this Hour.*

At last a British squadron with a relieving army stood off the Virginia coast, but it was too late. Cornwallis had sent a drummer boy in scarlet to sound "The Parley" on the British breastworks. The drum could not be heard over the cannonade, until a British officer at last stood up and waved a white handkerchief. This message was understood.

On October 19, 1781, the British regulars marched out of Yorktown, their fifes wailing *The World Turned Upside Down.* They marched through a mile-long column of French and Continentals, to stack arms, and enter captivity. Cornwallis did not appear; he sent an Irish brigadier to present his sword to Washington. The American general replied in kind, forcing the British officer to surrender to his own second-in-command. It was, as Lord North cried out when he heard the news, all over. The North Ministry fell; years of pushing an expensive, unpopular, and indecisive war had built up too much resentment and apathy in Britain. The British still had the power to fight America, but the official will to do so was at last broken.

It would take two more years to secure a treaty of peace, but the British would risk no more armies, and the end was in sight.

General Thomas Nelson received the highest praise from Washington for his conduct at Yorktown: *The general would be guilty of the highest ingratitude . . . if he forgot to return his sincere acknowledgments to his excellency governor Nelson . . . to whose activity, emulation and bravery, the highest praises are due.*

Now in quite poor health, Nelson resigned his office in favor of Benjamin Harrison, in November, 1781. But his sacrifices, although he had already exhausted his health and his fortune, were not quite over.

A hue and a cry followed him. His *activity, emulation and bravery* had been too much for some of his countrymen. During the last crisis, Nelson saw to it that the troops were cared for, fair means or foul. He impressed goods and rations by force, when there was no money to pay for them. He forced other citizens to take paper money—legal tender in the state—for supplies they refused to sell except for specie. The British did have hard money, and Nelson laid embargoes and dealt harshly with anyone caught selling supplies to Cornwallis. He did all these acts, so utterly necessary to assist an American victory, by executive action, and without having the warrants signed by the Council. The acts were thus illegal, and this was a great point seized upon by many Virginians who had hoped to avoid the war altogether until Nelson forced them to sacrifice for it. Charges were brought up against him in the legislature.

The legislature's answer was to pass an act of indemnity, forever absolving Governor Thomas Nelson, Jr., of any and all "official" crimes committed in the service of his country.

But the same act made no attempt to indemnify him for his personal losses. Nor did any future state or national legislature do so. The notes Nelson had signed to secure credit for the state fell due. Nelson's estates were forfeited. Whatever others might do, he paid his debts, *like an honest man*. He lost everything he owned, and retired to a small house in Hanover County with his wife and children. There were no more fox hunts or parties. As one biographer bitterly a few years afterward, *the vast estates were gone, honor and love remained*. Much later, there were eulogies, but Nelson was buried at York in an unmarked grave, at the age of fifty, and his widow, later, when in her eighties, blind, sick, and poor, still hoped for some official reimbursement.

Nelson, as a French visitor in his years of decline wrote, never complained. A Colonel Innis of Virginia said it better, quoting Shakespeare: *This was a man.*

Posterity Will Triumpl

The 56 men who signed the Declaration were by no means all leading patriots in the colonies. For example, two men who are often mistakenly believed to have signed, George Washington and Patrick Henry, certainly would have, but were engaged in vital business away from Philadelphia. Washington had been appointed to command the first American army; Henry was governor of his state. Similarly, in South Carolina and other colonies, leading men were waging the fundamental battle to bring their sections to the side of independence. The Marylanders such as Carroll and Paca thus were not in Congress to vote for independence, but having carried their colony for it, they arrived in time to sign.

The Signers did not then include all the American leadership of the Revolution, but they were a good cross-section of it. This fact was of extreme historic importance. The Continental Congresses, until July, 1776, at least, were extralegal under the ruling British law; they had no traditions or authority, and their entire prestige had to come from the kind of man who sat in them. This was recognized in most of the colonies, and many of the best men were sent. The fact that the delegations included Washingtons, Lees, Livingstons, and Adamses—in almost every case the most respected names in their home communities—gave Congress tremendous prestige and weight. At the time, this was vital. Later, when American laws and traditions were institutionalized, such a confluence of talent was desirable, but hardly necessary.

The times, condition, and spirit of eighteenth-century America threw up a spectacularly outstanding group of men. It was a group that continues to amaze not only foreign observers, but Americans themselves. The massed talent and intellect of a group that included Thomas Jefferson, George Wythe, James Wilson, Benjamin Franklin, John Adams, Richard Henry Lee, Oliver Wolcott, and John Witherspoon, to name just a few, was and is awesome. That these men accurately represented the best genius of the American people is not questioned; Jefferson and Franklin are ranked as men of true genius in competition with their entire world. The talents of men in the "second tier," such as Francis Hopkinson, are impressive.

These men not only declared independence, but a very

large portion of them went on to be instrumental in the founding of the Republic. They conceived and codified its laws and institutions. It is significant that Jefferson, who wrote and embodied the ideals in the Declaration, freely admitted that they were not just the result of his own genius, but the consensus viewpoint of the Congress.

Every old colony and new state, with the exception of Rhode Island—which already had a liberal constitution—and Connecticut, forged a new constitution and erected a new state government during the Revolutionary War. The Signers as individuals played a leading role in each of these developments. The ideals—and the changes due to experience—that were later written into the United States Constiution grew entirely out of the ground broken in the various states. And again, many of the same men who broke this ground in the several states went to the Constitutional Convention of 1787 and became the Founding Fathers. Other Signers, on the Federal bench, established important concepts and precedents, which took root as part of the organic national law.

It is not too much to state that the Signers—many of whom were very hesitant to break the ties that bound the colonies to Great Britain—as a body, set the new nation upon its future course. Their very reluctance to commit the first act was a reflection of their concern for the future. They recognized that a separation from the mother country demanded the formation of a new government, and they were extremely concerned with that new government's eventual shape and course.

That they did not want to preside over social revolution and chaos is evident from a study of any of the individual careers. They were socially conservative in their fashion.

They were not hostile to the "deferential society" that threw them upon America's stage, or the fundamental precepts of English civil right and law. A peculiar set of circumstances in America brought them forth. They wanted to continue most of the things about America they considered good. As in England, the local self-government on the county level that had grown up was the birthplace and the school for national democracy, just as the Continental Congress became the nursery for American statesmen, in John Adams' phrase.

The American Revolution, as any inspection of the lives of the Signers shows, was a series of rebellions against arbitary government, not society. Jefferson probably illustrated better than anyone else that government, any government, is often hostile to the desires and well-being of its people. A limitation of the powers of government—not only the British government, but all government—was fundamental to the Founding Fathers. At the same time, they recognized the possible dangers of mass government. Some states during the Revolution were subjected to such mass pressures, particularly on money matters, with disastrous results. By the end of the fighting, the most influential Signers had agreed that the eventual solution was representative, not mass, democracy. The peculiarly effective American system, which recognized that all power lay with the people but diffused real power between three branches of government, bicameral legislatures, and state and nation, was the result.

Almost all the later revolutions of the modern world differed fundamentally from the American. The French, Mexican, and Russian revolutions were waged not only against arbitrary government, but against an oppressive society itself. Their course was to forge a new, powerful regime, under new people, under which the real "revolution" could be carried out. This was the utter antithesis of the ideal of the Signers.

The American revolutionaries did not try to establish a government to carry out programs or ideological concepts, or even to solve the eternal question of "which people" should administrate the sovereign power, in the people's name. What they did was to establish government by consent. This was the underlying, and the genuine, principle of the entire Revolution. Taxation was merely an issue.

Government by consent was probably the most radical idea ever put forward by a dominant group of prominent men. It was, and remains, the fundamental basis of English-speaking democracy.

The American revolutionaries enjoyed one, sometimes overlooked, advantage: America in the main was an open society, and grinding poverty did not exist. Where it did, there were individual means of overcoming it, as the careers of Benjamin Franklin, Roger Sherman, and George Walton all attest.

The French, Mexican, and Russian Revolutions all contained certain hideous phenomena: terror, blood purges, deliberate and bitter class warfare, the rise of demagogues and opportunists to power, military regimes, and eventually, some form of state tyranny. Government, for better or worse, emerged as a stronger vehicle in the end. It is simplistic to say that there were no need for these things in eighteenth-century America. Demagogues did arise; class warfare did try to emerge in some regions, and there were opportunists aplenty. But the American Revolution, although it did have its seamier side with the persecution of

Tories, failed to produce guillotines or firing squads, and, above all, it brought forth no Napoleons or Lenins. The American leadership was determined this should not happen. In 1776, the American leadership actually made an American war against Great Britain rather than a "revolution" in the twentieth century sense.

Uniquely, the American revolt against Great Britain was begun, fostered, led, and finally triumphed under the same group of men, from start to finish. Radicalism did not destroy moderation, and fanaticism was never allowed to emerge. Significantly, Charles Carroll opposed the confiscation of Tory property throughout the war, and Middleton and Rutledge of South Carolina were extremely reluctant to punish Tories at its victorious end. Lewis Morris, Richard Henry Lee, and Thomas Nelson, Jr., were among many of the most influential leaders who risked everything, but insisted that private debts to British merchants be ultimately paid. These merchants did not cause the war, and most of them opposed actual British policy throughout the conflict. But it took a singularly ethical group of men to recognize the fact to their own personal detriment.

The honor, and ethical force, of the dominant Signers, was outstanding. George Wythe, who would not take a dishonorable case, gave concepts of immense value to the Revolution—but Thomas Nelson, who was no scholar nor any sort of intellectual, gave equally invaluable service, just by being his honest self. The Lees, Nelsons, Jeffersons—the list is long—were almost painfully high-minded men.

Socially conservative, they could not be accused of selfishness or reactionary sentiments. Although the Revolution began as an assertion of American right, with no aim of social change, the Signers fostered, presided over, and in many cases implemented far-reaching democratizations. Carter Braxton, the most reluctant of rebels, voted for the disestablishment of the Church as a Virginia legislator. Edward Rutledge eased out the rule of primogeniture in his state. Most of the Signers followed similar paths. They were inherently libertarian, if not enamoured with leveling or mass democracy. This intensely ethical leadership presided over the liquidation of many of their own privileges: entail, primogeniture, and the like. They laid a groundwork that allowed further democratization and change. The structure they built was so liberal, and at the same time so pragmatically conservative, that it became the only eighteenth-century government and Constitution to survive intact through modern times.

The merchants, lawyers, and landowners, that composed the Signers were acknowledged members of the "upper orders," as they were called. This requires some investigation of the Tory opposition during the Revolution. The conflict was never between the haves and have-nots in America; the Revolution never followed this course. The Tories, like the patriots, were drawn from all orders. Some fought for the Crown, not defending the Crown's actions or positions, out of a "Stuart" sense of loyalty, honorable and tragic figures. There were also local factors: in New England some prominent Anglicans chose the Crown out of opposition to the Congregational masses; and in New York small farmers up the Hudson opted for the royal governor because the bulk of the landed gentry of the province seemed against him. Similar reactions occurred in the South, among western farmers, who had long-standing conflicts with the tidewater-dominated, rebellious assemblies.

Judging from statements and private letters of Tories, a stronger sense of social snobbery prevailed among them; the concept of aristocracy was certainly deeper in old-wealthy families such as the Delanceys and Fairfaxes who choose the Crown. These people detested Republican sentiments. They seem to have been far more consciously élitist than the actual élite who assembled at Philadelphia—who held to the concept that the source of power and civil right was the people. Ironically, the most "élitist" groups in America, the Royalist circles, were not the actual power structure, which was found on the patriot side within the scattered assemblies. In choosing sides, social standing played some, but not a decisive, part.

Actually, the Tories were composed primarily of the "ins" among the propertied groups or officeholders, while the battlers in the assemblies had become the "outs." Men such as Thomas Hutchinson and William Franklin, the royal governors of Massachusetts and New Jersey, were Americans, along with hundreds of other appointive Crown officers. Their party, or more accurately, faction, was in power at the start of the conflict, and they remained stuck with it. It is a matter of record that Hutchinson, who lived out his life in exile in England, never felt comfortable in British circles, and some former Crown officials returned to America after the war.

Every man who took a seat in Congress and signed the Declaration was aware of two things: he was risking his life, property, and family; and republics traditionally are ungrateful. It took a stout heart as well as strong moral convictions to accept a post of leadership in 1776. Again, significantly, the majority of those who hoped for the emoluments and glory of office were on the royal side. And for the most part, although they were widely dispossessed and thousands chose exile at the end of the war, American Tories were generously rewarded by the Crown. The British government spent a phenomenal amount of money in their rehabilitation and relief, with land grants, awards, and pensions. While many Tories lost heavily because of the outcome of the war, no prominent Tory leaders suffered the complete ruin many of the Signers did.

The hardships of the American colonial experience, the spirit of seventeenth-century English liberties, the open lands, the self-reliance of a pioneer breed, and an unusual concern for education, already an American hallmark, all helped create an enlightened, courageous leadership in America. The political system that evolved on these shores, in the local legislatures, and the nature of the crisis—between the assemblies and the overseas government—threw this peculiarly American gentry-leadership into prominence and power. No man, in 1776, was likely to be sent to Congress to represent the whole unless he had first distinguished himself and was respected in his local community, because the delegates were chosen from among the leaders of the several assemblies. It was highly significant that most of these leaders were in government, or prominent in some way, before the actual crisis arose. Thus the Revolution did not spawn a newer, less palatable leadership. Equally important, this leadership did not shirk its ultimate duty, on the brink of crisis. If it had, the popular passions already aroused by their stands, and arguments among the people, to which Charles Carroll referred, would have thrown up new men to take their places. It is conceivable that adventurers—Benedict Arnold, brave, unsteady, amoral, was one—might have led the public through the war. Such men might also have leveled the rule of law, canceled courts and private debts alike, and produced a very different kind of society among the thirteen original states. America did not lack men of unrestrained violence, popular enough, but untrained in either government or law.

Obviously, almost none of the Signers had anything to gain personally by armed revolution, and the briefest investigation of their backgrounds shows that the vast majority had a tremendous amount to lose. Not all were born to wealth or advantage. But those who worked up to the apex of colonial society, such as Franklin, Sherman, Hewes, George Walton, and Thomas Jefferson, who came of yeoman stock, had gained as much as the greatest aristocrats through labor and talent. They had perhaps even more to lose.

But two things stand out among all the Signers: they were public-spirited, and they were patriotic, almost to a man.

At least two of the men who were reluctant to the end to vote for independence or to sign the Declaration should be mentioned. John Jay of New York, who did not sign, probably gained more for the new nation abroad than any other American, next to Franklin; he was instrumental in the advantageous peace of 1783. John Dickinson of Pennsylvania, who resigned rather than violate his judgment, enlisted in Washington's army as a private. He served with honor, became a brigadier general of Pennsylvania militia, and at the end of the Revolution was a highly respected man. There were many others of similar cut. They had their differences of viewpoint and strategy, but they were patriots at the core.

In fact, the actions of the Signers can be judged on no other basis, than that of patriotism. They had strong principles, but few, if any, were ideologues. When they signed, they were signing for their country, for then, and for posterity. Patriotism, rather than any form of politics, was their common cement.

Afterward, the Signers were a remarkably long-lived group. Those whom the war did not kill or injure lived beyond the normal span. Only a very few, like Francis Lightfoot Lee, John Penn of North Carolina, Thomas Nelson, and Abraham Clark of New Jersey, left public life or fell into obscurity. Half of all Signers served after the Revolution as president, state governors, state legislators, United States senators or representatives. Many found their way to the state and Federal benches. Only one man, William Ellery of Rhode Island, remained in a minor appointive post, as a collector of customs. John Adams and Thomas Jefferson became President in turn, and little Elbridge Gerry died in a coach on his way to the Senate, as Vice President under James Monroe.

Virtually all of these men had more wealth before they took up public office than when they left it. Robert Treat Paine of Massachusetts and John Penn of North Carolina, who had to leave office in order to support their families, and Thomas Jefferson, who was born in comfortable circumstances and married wealth, but neglected his private affairs while helping found a nation and died staving off bankruptcy, were highly typical. Most Signers would have been better off financially if they had never sat in Congress.

What did their act of courage and patriotism get the

Signers? At the end, *Love and honor remained.* The nation remained, too. That was all most of them asked.

The first Fourth of July was celebrated with *guns, bells, bonfires, and illuminations.* A terrible price was paid. Posterity has triumphed, as John Adams prayed; the glorious Fourth is still celebrated with pomp and parade, shows, games, and sports.

To make it so, 56 Americans pledged their lives, their fortunes, and their sacred honor.

It was no idle pledge. Nine Signers died of wounds or hardships during the Revolutionary War.

Five were captured or imprisoned, in some cases with brutal treatment.

The wives, sons, and daughters of others were killed, jailed, mistreated, persecuted, or left penniless. One was driven from his wife's deathbed and lost all his children.

The houses of twelve Signers were burned to the ground. Seventeen lost everything they owned.

Every Signer was proscribed as a traitor; every one was hunted. Most were driven into flight; most were at one time or another barred from their families or homes.

Most were offered immunity, freedom, rewards, their property, or the lives and release of loved ones to break their pledged word or to take the King's protection. Their fortunes were forfeit, but their honor was not. No Signer defected, or changed his stand, throughout the darkest hours. Their honor, like the nation, remained intact.

These men died, and most are almost forgotten by their countrymen. This does not really matter; men die and are forgotten. What does matter is that the country remember that freedom, on the first or any other Fourth of July, comes high.

Index